12.2.1986, M. Hinterseher

A FIELD GUIDE TO
AUSTRALIAN TREES

RIGBY FIELD GUIDE SERIES

Field Guide to Australian Birds Vol. 1 (Non-Passerines)
Field Guide to Australian Birds Vol. 2 (Passerines)
Field Guide to Australian Native Shrubs
Field Guide to Australian Trees
Field Guide to Australian Wildflowers Vol. 1
Field Guide to Australian Wildflowers Vol. 2
Field Guide to Banksias
Field Guide to the Marine Life of South-Eastern Australia
Field Guide to the National Parks of Victoria
Field Guide to Nests and Eggs of Australian Birds
Field Guide to the Tracks and Traces of Australian Animals
Gardener's Guide to Eucalypts

A FIELD GUIDE TO

AUSTRALIAN TREES

IVAN HOLLIDAY
RON HILL

Also by Ivan Holliday

Australian Shrubs in Colour
Eucalypts in Colour
Growing Australian Plants *(with Noel Lothian)*
Plants of the Flinders Ranges *(with Ron Hill)*
A Field Guide to Australian Native Shrubs *(with Geoffrey Watton)*
A Field Guide to Banksias *(with Geoffrey Watton)*
A Gardener's Guide to Eucalypts *(with Geoffrey Watton)*

National Library of Australia
Cataloguing-in-Publication entry

Holliday, Ivan, 1926–
　A field guide to Australian trees.

　Updated ed.
　Previous ed.: Adelaide; Rigby, 1983.
　Bibliography.
　Includes index.
　ISBN 0 7270 1999 6.

　1. Trees—Australia—Identification. I. Hill, Ron,
　1928–1974. II. Title.

582.160994

RIGBY PUBLISHERS • ADELAIDE
SYDNEY • MELBOURNE • BRISBANE • PERTH
NEW YORK • LONDON • AUCKLAND
First published 1969
Reprinted 1971, 1972
Revised (colour) edition 1974
Reprinted 1975, 1976, 1979, 1983
Updated edition 1984
Copyright © 1969 I. Holliday and R. Hill
All rights reserved
Wholly designed and typeset in Australia
Printed by Dai Nippon Printing Co. (H.K.) Ltd
　in Hong Kong

CONTENTS
Indexed as Common Names

Abergubber 156
Antarctic Beech 196
Australian Oak 118, 126
       Teak 146

Ball Nut 178
Bastard Tallow Wood 112
Bats-Wing Coral Tree 82
Bead Tree 192
Bean Tree 82
Beech Tree 196
Beefwood 154
Belah 66
Bell Fruit Tree 74
Berrigan 80, 202
Bitter Quandong 210
Black Bean 62
    Box 106
    Boy 170
    Gin 170
    Jack 34
    Oak 66
    Pine 206
    Sally 124
    Sheoak 70
    Tea-Tree 186
    Wattle 10

Blackbutt 112
Blackwood 16
Bloodwood 30, 84, 86, 90
Blue Fig 78
    Gum 102, 108
    Mallet 134
    Quandong 78
Blueberry Ash 78
Blue-Bush 130, 202
Blue-Fruited Lilly Pilly 218
Boobialla 194
Bottle-Brush 56
Box, 84, 108, 110, 136
Box-Leaf Wattle 18
Box Olive Wood 52
Bracelet Tree 78
Broad-Leaved Apple 30
    Paperbark 188
    Red Ironbark 136
Broughton Willow 22
Brown Mallet 134
    Pine 206
Brush Box 224
    Cherry 218
Budda 80
Bull Oak 64
Bullock Bush 166
Buloke 64

Bunya Pine 32
Bushy Sugar Gum 92
Bushy Yate 134

Cabbage Tree Palm 176
Cajuput Tree 188
Callaille 114
Candlebark 128
Celery Top Pine 36
Christmas Bush 52
       Tree 198
Coachwood 72
Coast Banksia 44, 46
       Wattle 14
Coastal Tea-Tree 174
Cooba 22
Coolabah 114
Coolibah 114
Coolgardie Gum 138
Cootamundra Wattle 6
Coral Gum 138
       Tree 82
Cork-Bark Tree 162
Cow-Itch Tree 172
Creek Lilly Pilly 218
Crow's Ash 146
Crowsfoot Elm 34
Cupania 76

Darwin Stringybark 116
Deep Yellow-Wood 208
Desert Kurrajong 50
       Oak 66
Dogwood 72
Drooping Myall 12, 26, 106
       Sheoak 68
Dundas Mahogany 130

Eumong 22
Eurabbie 102

Fern-Leaved Grevillea 156
Fig 144
Fire-Wheel Tree 214
Fire-Wood Banksia 42
Flame Grevillea 156
       Tree 48
Flat-Topped Yate 96, 134
Flooded Gum 88, 104
Forest Oak 70
Fragrant Sandalwood 210
Frangipani 168
Fringed Wattle 18

Ghost Gum 88, 122
Giant Banksia 40
       Mallee 120
Gidgee 8
Gimlet Gum 90, 100, 130, 132
Gippsland Waratah 220
Gnaingar 116
Golden Rain Wattle 18
       Wattle 20
       Wreath Wattle 24
Gosford Wattle 18
Gossamer Wattle 14
Grass-Leaved Hakea 160
Grass Tree 170
Green Cancer 10
Green-Leaved Moreton Bay Fig 142
Green Wattle 10
Grey Box 114
       Mangrove 38
       Teak 152

Hickory 16
Holly-Leaved Banksia 42
Honey Myrtle 180
Hoop Pine 32
Horse-Radish Tree 74
Huon Pine 36

Illawarra Flame Tree 48
Illawarra Plum 206
Illyarrie 98
Indian Coral Tree 82
Inland Paperbark 180
Ironbark 90, 110, 136
Ironwood 12

Jarrah 24, 28, 40, 86, 94, 170

Kangaroo Tea-Tree 184
Kanuka 224
Karri 28, 40, 86, 94, 170, 182
Kauri Pine 32
King William Pine 36
Kurrajong 50

Lacebark Tree 48
Lancewood 2
Lemon-Scented Gum 90
Leopard Wood 146, 148
Lilly Pilly 218
Lily of the Valley Tree 78
Lindsay Gum 100
Long-Flowered Marlock 96
Long-Leaved Emu Bush 80, 166

Maiden's Gum 102
Mallee 84
Mallet 134
Mallow 172
Mangrove 38

Manna Gum 128
Marlock 84
Marri 86
Melaleuca Gum 116
Merrit 120
Messmate 118, 126
Messmate Stringybark 118
Miljee 202
Mistletoe 198, 210
Mock Orange 204
Moonah 184, 186
Moreton Bay Chestnut 62
     Fig 142, 144
Morrel 130
Mountain Ash 84, 126
    Brown Pine 206
Mt Morgan Wattle 6
Mugga 136
Mulga 4, 8, 12
Mustard Tree 74
Myall 22

Narrow-Leaf Paperbark 190
Narrow-Leaved Red Ironbark 136
Native Apricot 202
  Box 52
  Cherry 140, 206
  Cypress Pine 58
  Frangipani 168
  Orange 8, 60
  Peach 210
  Poplar 74
  Willow 22, 106
Needle Hakea 162
Negrohead Beech 196
New South Wales Christmas Bush
    72
    Waratah 220
Norfolk Island Hibiscus 172

North Queensland White Beech 152

Oak 64
Octopus Tree 212
Oil Mallee 120
Orange Banksia 42
    Wattle 24

Paperbark 180-184, 188, 190
Peebeen 216
Peppermint 84
Pin Cushion Hakea 160
Pink Gum 108
Plum Bush 210
Poppel Nut 178
Port Gregory Gum 86
Port Jackson Fig 144
Powder-Barked Wandoo 84
Prickly-Leaf Paperbark 190
Punk Tree 188
Pyramid Tree 172

Quandong 78, 210
Queensland Kauri Pine 32
    Maple 146
    Nut 178
    Silver Wattle 6

Raspberry Jam Tree 2
Red Apple 218
    Box 110
    Cap Gum 98
    Cedar 222
    Ironbark 108, 136
    Mallee 120
    Morrel 120
    Stringybark 136
Red-Leaved Palm 176

Redwood 36, 120
River Banksia 46
    Box 106
    Cooba 22
    Oak 64
    Red Gum 22, 88, 122, 128, 176
Rose Gum 104
    Sheoak 70
Rosewood 166
Rough-Barked Apple 30
Rush-Leaf Grevillea 156
Rusty-Leaved Fig 144

Salmon Gum 130, 132
Salt Bush 148
Salt River Mallet 134
    Yate 134
Sandalwood 140, 194, 210
Sand Mallee 96, 134
Saw Banksia 44
Scented Satinwood 72
Screw Palm 200
    Pine 200
Scrub Beefwood 158, 214
    Wilga 150
Sheoak 64
Sheoke 68
She Pine 206
Silky Oak 156, 158
Silver Banksia 44
Silver-Topped Gimlet 132
Silver Wattle 6, 10
Small Cooba 22
Small-Fruited Queensland Nut 178
Small-Leaved Cork Bark 162
    Fig 144
    Water Gum 218
Smooth-Barked Apple 30
Snow Gum 124

South Australian Blue Gum 108
    Paperbark 184
Southern Blue Gum 102
Spotted Gum 90
Stringybark 84, 94, 118
Stinking Wattle 8
Sugar Gum 92
Sugarwood 80, 166, 194
Swamp Banksia 46
    Mallet 134
    Oak 64, 66
    Paperbark 182
    Yate 134
Sweet Bursaria 52
    Pittosporum 204
Sydney Apple 30
    Blue Gum 70, 104, 112
    Golden Wattle 14

Tallow Wood 112
Tanglefoot 196
Tasmanian Blue Gum 102
    Oak 118, 126
    Waratah 220
Tea-Tree 174, 180
Toona Tree 222
Tree Waratah 220
Tulip Oak 34
    Satinwood 208
Tulipwood 164
Turpentine Tree 216

Umbrella Bush 22
    Mulga 4
    Tree 34, 212

Wandoo 84
Waratah 220
Waratah Banksia 42
Warty Yate 134
Water Bush 154
Water Gum 224
Wattle 2
Weeping Bottle-Brush 54, 56
    Myrtle 218
    Willow 22, 28
Western Australian Christmas Tree 198
    Red Flowering Gum 86, 116
    Sheoak 68
    Willow Myrtle 28
Western Myall 26
Wheel of Fire Tree 214
White Beech 152
    Bottle-Brush 54
    Cedar 192
    Cypress Pine 58
    Kurrajong 48
    Mallee 100
    Paperbark 182
    Sallow Wattle 14
    Sally 124
    Silky Oak 158
    Tree 188
Wild Orange 60
Wilga 148, 150
Willow Wattle 24
Woollybutt 116

Yarran 8
Yate 134
Yate Gum 134
Yathoo 114
Yellow Box 110, 136
    Gum 108, 136
Yorrel 120

CONTENTS
Indexed as Botanical Names

Abutilon 172
Acacia 2, 10, 20, 130
Acacia acuminata 2
    aneura 4, 12
    baileyana 6
    brachystachya 4
    buxifolia 18
    cambagei 8
    cyanophylla 24
    dealbata 6, 10
    decurrens 10
    doratoxylon 2
    estrophiolata 12
    excelsa 12
    fimbriata 18
    floribunda 14
    gillii 20
    homalophylla 8
    implexa 16
    ligulata 22
    loderi 26
    longifolia 14
    mearnsii 10
    melanoxylon 16
    normalis 10
    oswaldii 202
    papyrocarpa 22, 26
    pendula 12, 22, 26, 106
    podalyriifolia 6
    prominens 18
    pycnantha 20
    salicina 22, 106
    saligna 24
    sophorae 14
    sowdenii 26
    stenophylla 22

Agathis robusta 32
Agonis 28
Agonis flexuosa 28
    juniperina 28

Anacardiaceae 208
Anacardium 76
Angophora 30

Angophora costata 30
    floribunda 30
    intermedia 30
    lanceolata 30
    subvelutina 30

Araliaceae 212
Araucaria 32
Araucaria bidwillii 32
    cunninghamii 32
Araucariaceae 32
Argyrodendron 34
Argyrodendron actinophyllum 34
    trifoliatum 34
Athrotaxis cupressoides 36

Athrotaxis selaginoides 36
Avicennia 38
Avicennia marina 38
        officinalis 38

Banksia 40, 56
Banksia attenuata 46
     coccinea 42
     grandis 40
     ilicifolia 42
     integrifolia 44
     littoralis 46
     littoralis var.
        seminuda 46
     marginata 44
     menziesii 42
     prionotes 42
     serrata 44
     verticillata 46
Bipinnatae 10
Boronia 146
Brachychiton 48
Brachychiton acerifolium 48
        discolor 48
        gregorii 50
        hybrida 48
        populneum 50
Brassaia actinophylla 212
Bursaria 52
Bursaria incana 52
     spinosa 52

Callistemon 54, 56
Callistemon salignus 54
        viminalis 56
Callitris 58
Callitris columellaris 58
Capparidaceae 60
Capparis 60
Capparis mitchellii 60
Castanospermum australe 62

Casuarina 64
Casuarina acutivalvis 68
     cristata 66
     cunninghamiana 64
     decaisneana 66
     fraserana 68
     glauca 64, 66
     leuhmanni 64
     littoralis 70
     stricta 68
     suberosa 70
     torulosa 70
Casuarinaceae 64-70
Cedrela toona var. *australis* 222
Ceratopetalum 72
Ceratopetalum apetalum 72
        corymbosum 72
        gummiferum 72
        succirubrum 72
        virchowii 72
Choricarpia 216
Codonocarpus australis 74
        cotinifolius 74
        pyramidalis 74
Correa 146
Cunoniaceae 72
Cupaniopsis 76
Cupaniopsis anacardioides 76
Cupressaceae 58

Dacrydium franklinii 36

Elaeocarpaceae 78
Elaeocarpus cyaneus 78
     grandis 78
     obovatus 78
     reticulatus 78
Eremophila 80, 130

Eremophila longifolia 80, 166
    mitchellii 80
Eriostemon 146
Erythrina indica 82
    phlebocarpa 82
    variegata 82
    vespertilio 82
Eucalyptus 30, 84, 90, 116, 130
Eucalyptus accedens 84
    astringens 134
    bicolor 106
    bicostata 102
    brockwayi 130
    calophylla 86
    camaldulensis 88, 122
    campaspe 132
    citriodora 90
    cladocalyx 92
    cladocalyx 'Nana' 92
    cornuta 134
    crebra 136
    diversicolor 94
    eremophila 96, 134
    erythrocorys 98
    erythronema 100
    erythronema var.
      marginata 100
    fasciculosa 108
    fibrosa 136
    ficifolia 86, 116
    flocktoniae 120
    foecunda 120
    gardneri 134
    globulus 102
    gracilis 130
    grandis 88, 104
    largiflorens 106
    lehmanii 134
    leucoxylon 108, 136
    leucoxylon var.
      macrocarpa 108
    leucoxylon 'Rosea' 108
    longicornis 120
    macrandra 96
    macrorhyncha 136
    maculata 90
    maidenii 102
    marginata 94
    megacornuta 134
    melliodora 110, 136
    microcorys 112
    microtheca 114
    miniata 116
    niphophila 124
    obliqua 118, 126
    occidentalis 96, 134
    oleosa 120
    oleosa var. *glauca* 120
    oleosa var. *plenissima*
      120
    papuana 88, 122
    pauciflora 124
    pauciflora var. *alpina* 124
    phoenicea 116
    pilularis 112
    planchoniana 112
    polyanthemos 110
    redunca 84
    redunca var. *elata* 84
    regnans 126
    rubida 128
    rudis 88
    saligna 70, 104, 112
    salmonophloia 130, 132
    salubris 90, 130, 132
    sargentii 134
    sideroxylon 136
    sideroxylon 'Rosea' 136
    socialis 120
    spathulata 134
    stellulata 124
    st johnii 102

Eucalyptus tectifica 114
    tetrodonta 116
    torquata 138
    'Torwood' 138
    transcontinentalis 120
    viminalis 128
    wandoo 84
Eucarya acuminata 210
Eugenia brachyandra 218
    smithii 218
Exocarpos 140, 206
Exocarpos cupressiformis 140
    sparteus 140

Fagaceae 196
Fagus 196
Ficus 142
Ficus eugenioides 144
    macrophylla 142
    obliqua 144
    rubiginosa 144
    rubiginosa 'Variegata' 144
    watkinsiana 142
Flindersia 146
Flindersia australis 146
    brayleyana 146
    maculosa 146, 148
    strzeleckiana 146

Geijera 150
Geijera parviflora 148, 150
    salicifolia 150
Gmelina 152
Gmelina dalrympleana 152
    fasciculiflora 152
    leichhardtii 152
    macrophylla 152
Grevillea 154, 156, 160
Grevillea chrysodendron 156
    eriostachya 156
    excelsior 156
    hilliana 158
    juncifolia 156
    nematophylla 154
    pteridifolia 156
    robusta 156, 158
    striata 154

Hakea 154, 160
Hakea divaricata 162
    francisiana 160
    intermedia 162
    laurina 160
    leucoptera 162
    lorea 162
    suberea 162
Harpullia pendula 164
Heterodendrum oleaefolium 166
Hibiscus 172
Hymenosporum 168
Hymenosporum flavum 168

Kingia australis 170

Lagunaria 172
Lagunaria patersonii 172
Leguminosae 2-26, 62, 82
Leptospermum 174
Leptospermum laevigatum 174
    scoparium 174
Liliaceae 170
Livistona 176
Livistona australis 176
    mariae 176
Loranthaceae 198

Macadamia 178
Macadamia integrifolia 178
    praealta 178

Macadamia ternifolia 178
Malvaceae 172
Melaleuca 54, 56, 180, 188
Melaleuca alternifolia 190
    cajuputii 188
    cuticularis 182
    cymbifolia 182
    dissitiflora 190
    glomerata 180
    halmaturorum 184
    lanceolata 184, 186
    leucadendra 188
    linariifolia 190
    parviflora 186
    preissiana 182, 186
    pubescens 186
    quinquenervia 188
    rhaphiophylla 182
    styphelioides 190
    trichostachya 190
    viridiflora 188
Melia azedarach var. *australasica* 192
Meliaceae 192, 222
Moraceae 142, 144
Myoporaceae 80, 194
Myoporum 194
Myoporum insulare 194
    platycarpum 80, 166, 194
Myrtaceae 28, 30, 54, 56, 84-138, 174, 180-190, 216, 218, 224

Nothofagus 196
Nothofagus cunninghamii 196
    gunnii 196
    moorei 196
Nuytsia 210
Nuytsia floribunda 198

Palmae 176
Pandanaceae 200
Pandanus 200
Pandanus aquaticus 200
    basedowii 200
    pedunculatus 200
    spiralis 200
Phyllocladus asplenifolius 36
Phytolaccaceae 74
Pittosporaceae 52, 168, 202, 204
Pittosporum 168, 202
Pittosporum phylliraeoides 202, 204
    revolutum 204
    rhombifolium 204
    undulatum 204
Podocarpaceae 206
Podocarpus 206
Podocarpus alpina 206
    amarus 206
    elatus 206
    lawrencei 206
Proteaceae 40-46, 154-162, 178, 214, 220

Rhizophora 38
Rhodosphaera rhodanthema 208
Rutaceae 146, 148, 150

Salix 22, 28
Santalaceae 140, 210
Santalum acuminatum 210
    lanceolatum 210
    murrayanum 210
    spicatum 210
Sapindaceae 76, 164, 166
Schefflera actinophylla 34, 212
Sequoia sempervirens 36
Stenocarpus salignus 214
    sinuatus 214

Sterculiaceae 34, 48, 50
Syncarpia 216
Syncarpia glomulifera 216
         hillii 216
         laurifolia 216
         leptopetala 216
         procera 216
         subargentea 216
Syzygium coolminianum 218
         floribundum 218
         leuhmannii 218
         paniculatum 218

Taxodiaceae 36
Telopea oreades 220
         speciosissima 220
         truncata 220
Toona australis 222
Tristania conferta 224
         laurina 224
         neriifolia 224

Verbenaceae 38, 152

Xanthorrhoea 170

INTRODUCTION

When one considers that there are over five hundred Eucalyptus trees alone that are endemic to this country, and that in one square kilometre of virgin Queensland rain forest, over one hundred different species may be found, it becomes obvious that a book such as this cannot possibly include a comprehensive coverage of the trees of Australia.

An attempt has been made, however, to describe and illustrate trees from every part of the continent, from every environment. Perhaps there has been a preference for trees found in the arid inland. No apology is made for this, as many of these trees have received little attention in previous publications; but most important, they grow in areas where every tree, or living bush for that matter, should be carefully preserved.

If in this book, the already awakening public interest in our uniquely beautiful but disappearing Australian flora has been stimulated, then its purpose has been achieved.

RASPBERRY JAM TREE

Acacia acuminata Benth.　　　　　　　　　　　LEGUMINOSAE

Native only to Western Australia. "Raspberry Jam Tree" was very prevalent before the land was cleared and gives the name "Jam Country" to much of the best wheat land between Geraldton and the south coast.

The genus *Acacia* comprises over six hundred recorded species, all but a very few being endemic to Australia. These consist of trees and shrubs of all sizes to prostrate ground cover plants.

"Raspberry Jam Tree" is a "Wattle," as it is known in Australia; it loses its true compound leaves (feathery or bipinnate) as it develops to maturity. These are replaced by phyllodes which are really flattened leaf stalks. Phyllodes appear in many shapes and sizes on different species of *Acacia*, from small and rounded to long and narrow, or needle-like, and look exactly like simple, true leaves.

The tree is only small, **seldom more than 8 m high, but sometimes reaching 14 m,** with an umbrageous crown, slightly drooping. **Phyllodes** are long and narrow, bright shiny green, and the young shoots silky. **Bark** is fissured, smooth, and light grey.

It flowers in early spring producing masses of 2·5 cm long, deep yellow, rod-shaped **inflorescences** in thick clusters. All species of *Acacia* have either these rod-shaped (cylindrical spikes), or ball-shaped (globular) inflorescences, consisting of numerous, closely compacted stamens, varying in colour from cream to a deep orange-yellow.

Acacia seed, contained in small bean-like **pods,** is black and shiny and coated with a very hard outer covering (testa) which keeps the seed viable for a long period of time.

The name "Raspberry Jam" is derived from the smell of the wood when cut, which is fragrant like that of raspberry jam.

This is an ornamental, small flowering tree, suitable for cultivating in areas of moderate rainfall. It prefers well-drained, non-limy soils, but is adaptable.

LANCEWOOD *A. doratoxylon* A. Cunn. is an ornamental, dry area tree from all mainland States, which is similar in appearance to *A. acuminata.*

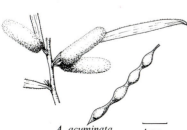
A. acuminata 1 cm

A. doratoxylon

MULGA

Acacia aneura F. Muell. LEGUMINOSAE

"Mulga" is a tree of the arid Inland. It is found over an extensive range in all States except Victoria and Tasmania.

The term "Mulga" is one frequently used by Australians when referring to any piece of scrubland, although, in fact, "Mulga" scrub is never seen near any of the major cities.

In the wetter parts of its habitat range, it sometimes occurs in dense thickets that are hard to penetrate; elsewhere it is often scattered throughout open country. Soils can be red sand dunes, stony or rocky, or, more usually, heavy clays subjected to flooding after heavy rains which often do not fall for several years at a time.

The tree is only small, **5 m** or less, to **10 m in height** at its best, with an umbrella-like crown, but extremely variable both in habit and foliage. The foliage is usually silvery grey, and the **inflorescences** deep yellow and rod-shaped. Flowering time is variable according to rainfall.

Phyllodes are variable, sometimes almost round, but often long and narrow, curved or straight. The **seed pods** are glabrous, broad, and flat, 1–4 cm long.

"Mulga" **wood** is well known for its use in the ornamental souvenir trade where it is cut and highly polished to show its characteristic, hard dark brown and yellow grain.

For many centuries the "Mulga" has survived the harsh drought-stricken areas of inland Australia, often where man and beast are unable to survive. Yet today it faces its deadliest enemy, man himself. Like other trees of the same arid regions, "Mulga" is a very necessary part of nature's balance. It is an excellent fodder tree, and, over the years, the running of stock in these parts has had a marked effect on tree life. The subsequent loss of tree cover in some parts is alarming.

"Mulga" is long lived and well worth cultivating in dry areas. The extra watering given to cultivated trees produces more regular flowering.

UMBRELLA MULGA *A. brachystachya* Benth. is a very similar small tree **to 7 m,** but always has narrow **phyllodes.** The **seed pods** are different from those of *A. aneura*, being woody and covered with fine hairs.

A. aneura   seed   *A. brachystachya*

1cm

COOTAMUNDRA WATTLE

Acacia baileyana F. Muell. LEGUMINOSAE

An original inhabitant of a very limited area of southern New South Wales in the Cootamundra and Wagga districts, "Cootamundra Wattle" is probably the most commonly cultivated of all the wattle trees—in Australia, at least.

Because of its lovely silvery blue foliage it is often called "Silver Wattle," although another species, *A. dealbata*, has been assigned this common name. Seldom, if ever, seen in its original habitat, the tree has sometimes regenerated so well elsewhere from planted specimens, that it could almost be considered a native of these areas.

This is a very beautiful species for the first 10–15 years of its rather short life span. It grows rapidly and is pyramidal in the early stages with branches to ground level, but later reverts to a dense, rounded crown supported by a short **trunk. Leaves** are small and feathery, composed of numerous, finely divided pinnae at right angles to the leaf stalk, and a mealy blue in colour. The smaller **branches** too, are glaucous, and the trunk and main branches persist in this same colouring for a number of years, but later turn grey as they age.

In flower it is spectacular, simply loaded down in mid-winter by numerous trusses of small, fluffy yellow **flower balls.** Unfortunately they are sometimes spoilt by rain.

The tree's relatively short life span can, to some extent, be prolonged by judicious pruning each year after flowering, to promote vigorous new growth.

In spite of these drawbacks this is a beautiful species, both for foliage and flowers, and has proved its popularity over the years. It is best planted in moist, acid soils in cool, hilly locations, where it can be allowed to regenerate naturally among other trees, particularly on the large estates, although it is adaptable and easily grown in other situations.

QUEENSLAND SILVER WATTLE or MT MORGAN WATTLE
A. podalyriifolia A. Cunn. is another often cultivated tree with lovely mealy-blue foliage. This species, however, belongs to the group with **phyllodes,** these being broad and rounded on this particular tree. It is **long flowering** from May to July, is not unduly rain spoilt and is a lovely sight in full bloom. This is a very beautiful species, best suited to non-limy soils.

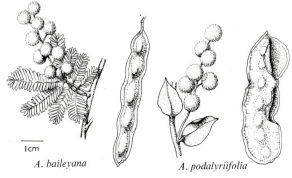

1cm

A. baileyana *A. podalyriifolia*

GIDGEE, STINKING WATTLE

Acacia cambagei R. T. Baker.   LEGUMINOSAE

"Gidgee" is native to the dry areas of inland temperate Australia, but does not extend into Western Australia. Where it occurs it is often the dominant tree, particularly when found along watercourses and in clay depressions where water collects after rain. Under these conditions it forms pure stands of dense scrub with interlacing branches, often bordering the treeless gibber plains.

At its best it forms a handsome and dense tree **up to 10 m in height**, with a wide-spreading, drooping crown. Under harsher conditions it is only **5–7 m high** with a sparse, open-canopied habit, and is usually associated with other plants such as "Mulga," "Native Orange," etc.

In keeping with many plants of the Inland, the foliage is grey coloured, the phyllodes being covered with a greyish-white scurf. At the approach of rain, or when wet, the foliage emits a particularly offensive smell that can be almost unbearable. The **phyllodes** are lanceolate, with a curved mucro (point) up to 15 cm long, with many fine striate nerves. **Bark** is dark brown, rough, and deeply furrowed. The **flowers** are not profuse, and are not a conspicuous feature of the tree. **Seed pods** are glabrous, and rather flat.

The **timber** is very hard and heavy, with a close, interlocked grain. It is noted for its durability and resistance to termites, and, among other things, is used extensively for fence posts. It is also an excellent firewood.

YARRAN *A. homalophylla* A. Cunn. is a close species often confused with "Gidgee." It has shorter **phyllodes** and different **seed pods** and seed arrangement, although "Gidgee" is mainly distinguished by the unpleasant smell of its foliage at certain times.

"Yarran" is also an inland tree, commonly encountered in the dry western plains of Queensland, Victoria and New South Wales. Its hard **timber** is fragrant and has many uses, particularly in the manufacture of tobacco pipes.

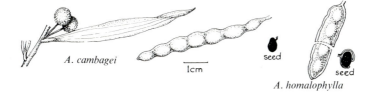

A. cambagei

1cm

A. homalophylla

BLACK WATTLE

Acacia decurrens Willd. LEGUMINOSAE

"Black Wattle" is a tree growing up to **14 m high** usually found in the cool, moist hills and gullies of many parts of southern and eastern Australia.

The tree belongs to the large group of the *Acacia* family known as *Bipinnattae*, i.e., those possessing feathery or bipinnate true leaves throughout their life span. This group includes many trees and shrubs which, with a few exceptions, inhabit the wetter zones of the continent (over 500 mm rainfall).

"Black Wattle" is a graceful, handsome tree with rich green feathery foliage and smooth green smaller **branches,** but dark grey, almost black main **trunk.** Often spreading when given room, it is more commonly erect, and rather slender among other trees. The showy racemes of globular, yellow **flower heads** arise from the leaf axils in great profusion in late winter, when the trees are a delight to behold. **Seed pods** 5–10 cm long, are flattened, slightly curved, and constricted between the seeds.

This species, once extensively planted for tanbark in South Africa, is now out of control in that country, and known as the "Green Cancer."

The species known as *A. normalis* is only another form of *A. decurrens.*

GREEN WATTLE *A. mearnsii* Willd. is a closely related species native to the same regions, but often occurring on poorer soil types. It is easily distinguished by its softer, pubescent foliage, shorter, broader **leaflets,** and pale **flowers** which appear in summer. It is also grown extensively in South Africa and elsewhere for its very valuable tanbark.

SILVER WATTLE *A. dealbata* Link. is another commonly cultivated tree, rather similar, but with a mealy powder on the **leaves** and smaller **branches** giving a silvery effect. The **flowers,** which are a pale lemon, appear about the same time as those of *A. decurrens.*

All species mentioned are ornamental trees, particularly when young. They can be grown in drier conditions but their life span and beauty are considerably increased if planted in cool, moist situations akin to their natural environment.

A. decurrens

1cm

IRONWOOD

Acacia estrophiolata F. Muell. LEGUMINOSAE

"Ironwood" is a dry area, inland tree, occurring in the north of South Australia west of Oodnadatta, and fairly commonly in central Australia.

The common name of "Ironwood" is applied to several other Australian trees, all of which possess a very hard **timber.** This tree is no exception, although the timber is perhaps no harder than that of "Mulga," and other inland acacias, with which it is associated.

It is usually a long-lived tree, and a series of growth stages takes place before its final form is attained. During the first years of its life it is a rather prickly, unattractive shrub. As it develops it becomes a small, dense tree, finally becoming a mature, weeping specimen, **about 10 m high.** The long, pendulous, branching habit makes this tree a conspicuous and beautiful feature of certain parts of the central Australian landscape.

The foliage is a light grey-green, **phyllodes** being fairly long (5–8 cm), narrow, and glabrous. **Flower heads** are globular, small, and not a conspicuous feature of the tree. **Seed pods** are rather narrow and flat, the seeds disc-shaped.

"Ironwood" is usually found in heavy clay soils where it can be seen as a stately, single specimen tree, or in groups, or sometimes as colonies. These colonies are especially prevalent in the flats and depressions between ranges of hills where any run-off from the very infrequent rains is collected.

There are some particularly fine specimens of the "Ironwood" in and around Alice Springs. To see these trees silhouetted against the fading light of day is a never-to-be-forgotten sight.

This tree would make a fine street or avenue tree for inland towns. In many respects it resembles the "Drooping Myall" (*A. pendula*).

Acacia excelsa Benth., also known as "Ironwood," is a similar tree growing **to 20 m,** and is one of the largest trees of the dry western plains of New South Wales and Queensland. This too is a particularly ornamental tree for dry conditions. In appearance it can be mistaken for the "Mulga" (*A. aneura*) described on p. 4.

SYDNEY GOLDEN WATTLE
Acacia longifolia Willd. LEGUMINOSAE

"Sydney Golden Wattle" is usually only a small tree common in the coastal division of New South Wales and extending to the tablelands, but also native to southern Queensland, Victoria and Tasmania. It is also found in the wetter parts of South Australia, such as the Mount Lofty Ranges, but has naturalised itself in these parts from original plantings.

This is a variable species, sometimes seen as a slender tree in shaded woodland or as a large bushy shrub, or when single specimens are given room to expand, it sometimes sprawls to a remarkable spread of 10 m or more in diameter, with branches along the ground.

It can be a very handsome ornamental small tree up **to 10 m in height** with a dense, bushy crown, and bright green, shiny foliage, paler at the young tips. **Phyllodes** are long (7–15 cm), rather broadly lanceolate or obovate, striped, with prominent longitudinal veins. The **bark** on the **trunk** and **main branches** is smoothish and a dull grey. The lemon-coloured **flowers** occur in large, fluffy, cylindrical spikes up to 5 cm long, prolific in August. **Seed pods** are curled and twisted.

When seen at its best this is a particularly ornamental species. It prefers moist, acid soils and although easily grown in other conditions seldom produces the healthy green foliage that contrasts so well with the flowers.

COAST WATTLE *A. sophorae* R.Br. is a coastal species which inhabits the coastal sand dunes of most of temperate Australia. Although only a sprawling, shrubby plant it is particularly useful as a sand binder and should be cultivated in seaside gardens. The **phyllodes** are rather thick and fleshy, but otherwise it is much the same as *A. longifolia*.

GOSSAMER WATTLE, WHITE SALLOW WATTLE *A. floribunda* Sieb. is another ornamental tree growing **to 14 m** which is closely related. It inhabits streams and moist gullies in the New South Wales and Queensland coastal areas, often on rich alluvial soils. It is usually a shapelier tree than *A. longifolia* with narrower drooping foliage and masses of pale yellow or cream **flower spikes** in early spring.

A. longifolia   *A. sophorae*   *A. floribunda*

BLACKWOOD

Acacia melanoxylon R. Br. LEGUMINOSAE

"Blackwood" is a forest tree mainly found in the cool, moist, temperate regions of south-eastern Australia but also extending to a sub-tropical climate in northern New South Wales and southern Queensland. It is found in the Mount Lofty Ranges and the wetter parts of the south-east in South Australia, over practically the whole of Tasmania, and in Victoria, New South Wales, and Queensland. Usually it is found as an understorey species to the large eucalypt forests where rainfall is 750–1800 mm annually.

It can be a fine, erect tree **25–30 m high, but more often 16 m or less,** with a **trunk** 30–100 cm in diameter. The **branches** begin well down the main trunk, are horizontal or slightly pendulous, and culminate in a dense rounded crown, the overall effect being very handsome. **Bark** is dark grey, rough, and furrowed, persistent to the smaller **branches.** **Phyllodes** are long and curved, bluntly pointed but tapering to the base, dark to pale green and leathery, with rather prominent longitudinal veins. The cream **flower balls** are in short axillary racemes, and appear in September. **Seed pods** are brown, flattened, and contorted, the black seeds within encircled by a bright red doubly folded funicle.

"Blackwood" **timber** is a prized fancy hardwood and is much sought after as a veneer for furniture and other decorative purposes. It is usually a dark brown colour, and frequently beautifully figured. The main source of "Blackwood' timber is Tasmania, but even there it is now in limited supply.

The tree favours deep, moist soils in a cool to mild climate. Under such conditions it forms a handsome, shapely specimen tree well worth cultivating as an ornamental evergreen.

HICKORY *A. implexa* Benth. is a very similar tree that grows in similar locations. Its **leaves** are more pointed, the **branches** more rounded, and the **seed funicles** pale coloured and folded under the seed where they are attached to the pod, but otherwise very difficult to distinguish from the "Blackwood" tree.

A. melanoxylon A. implexa

GOSFORD WATTLE, GOLDEN RAIN WATTLE

Acacia prominens A. Cunn.　　　　　　　　　　LEGUMINOSAE

"Gosford Wattle" is a lovely small to medium-sized tree native only to the east coast of New South Wales in the Sydney to Gosford districts.

Because of its ornamental appearance, however, it has found its way into cultivation, and is a reasonably well-known species in other places where climate is suitable.

The tree is quite variable as regards size, sometimes only reaching about **5 m in height,** but forming a fine, erect, well-branched tree of up **to 25 m** on the more fertile soils of adequate rainfall. It has an upright, smooth grey, but short **trunk,** and is well clothed with light grey-green rather silvery foliage, which is decorative at all times. The small slender racemes of **flowers** occur in early spring when the whole tree is covered in billowing masses of pale gold.

Phyllodes are 2·5–5 cm long, rather narrow, and slightly curved. **Seed pods** are straight, very flat, up to 10 cm long and a bluish colour.

This species does well as far south as Adelaide but prefers non-alkaline soils of assured rainfall. Under such conditions it should be more commonly cultivated than it is.

FRINGED WATTLE *A. fimbriata* A. Cunn. is a closely related species that is often found along river banks and in shady gullies in New South Wales and southern Queensland. It is equally as attractive as "Gosford Wattle," but **seldom** grows any **larger than 5–7 m high.** The foliage is a darker green, narrow and dainty, with a slightly drooping, lacy effect. The pale lemon **flower balls** are prolific and very beautiful. This species is adaptable and grows well in most soils receiving moderate rainfall.

BOX-LEAF WATTLE *A. buxifolia* A. Cunn. is another related and beautiful species with glaucous box-like **phyllodes** and deep yellow **flowers,** but which is usually only a shrub seldom exceeding **3 m in height.** It is found in Queensland, New South Wales, and Victoria.

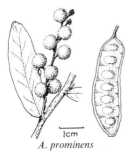
A. prominens
1cm

A. fimbriata

A. buxifolia

GOLDEN WATTLE

Acacia pycnantha Benth. LEGUMINOSAE

Of all the species of *Acacia* that enliven the Australian bushland and roadsides after a drab winter "Golden Wattle" perhaps rightly deserves top billing, at least in southern temperate Australia. This species is Australia's floral emblem.

The tree is not found in Western Australia but is very prevalent throughout the temperate regions of South Australia and Victoria where rainfall is at least 350 mm and up to 1000 mm annually. It is also native to the extreme south-west of New South Wales but has naturalised itself in the lower Tablelands of that State. It regenerates very freely, particularly after fire, and frequently occurs in dense thickets forming spindly plants as an understorey to eucalypt forest, or as a soil binder on denuded roadside cuttings. It is often seen at its best on very poor soils.

"Golden Wattle" is only a small tree, or sometimes a shrub, seldom exceeding about **8 m in height.** The **trunk** is short and thin, the crown umbrageous, with rather upright **branches. Bark** is dark brown and rather smooth. It is extremely valuable for its tanning properties and has been extensively cultivated for this purpose, particularly overseas.

The **phyllodes** appear at a very early age when they are particularly broad and large. Later they revert to a sickle or curved shape (falcate), rather broad, but variable, leathery, and shining, a bright green in colour.

The large racemes of deep yellow, fluffy **flower balls** are highly perfumed, and occur on thick stalks. They are prominently displayed and very striking when massed above the glossy green foliage. **Seed pods** are 7–12 cm long by 6 mm broad, dark brown, and slightly constricted between the seeds.

Although often a magnificent bush specimen, "Golden Wattle" does not take kindly to cultivation where it is frequently the subject of gall attack and does not flower well. It grows very rapidly with usually only a short life when cultivated.

A. gillii, Maiden et Blakely, is a South Australian species from Eyre Peninsula with very narrow **phyllodes** but otherwise very similar to *A. pycnantha*.

A. pycnantha   1cm

NATIVE WILLOW, COOBA, BROUGHTON WILLOW
Acacia salicina Lindl. LEGUMINOSAE

"Native Willow" has an extensive range in the dry inland regions of all mainland States where it is found, from tropical Western Australia to north-west Victoria. The tree favours watercourses or clay depressions, but is found on most soils of the low rainfall areas. It **seldom exceeds 14 m,** but in places grows to a large willow-like tree, 28 m tall.

As its common name implies, it is a tree with a drooping, willowy habit, which is very beautiful. One wonders why this tree is not used more as a substitute for the very vigorously rooted "Weeping Willow" (*Salix*). Although not deciduous, it is just as beautiful, and less troublesome. The tree is relatively slow growing and not so attractive in its early stages, features which probably restrict its popularity.

"Native Willow" has a shapely, rounded crown, with **branches** which droop to near ground level, providing ample shade. The **bark** is brown, or grey, smooth and fissured. **Phyllodes** are long and narrow (up to 20 cm) and rather fleshy. The cream **flowers** are not a conspicuous feature of the tree.

The tree suckers freely from the roots and is a useful soil binder in arid parts, although this feature is not a nuisance in cultivation.

It is a lovely, ornamental, and long-lived species, which will grow in most soils, and can withstand long periods without rain. Along with the "Myalls" (*A. pendula* and *A. papyrocarpa*) it possesses a rare Australian beauty that is seldom appreciated, at least for garden planting. When fully grown it makes a fine and permanent specimen or street tree.

UMBRELLA BUSH, SMALL COOBA *A. ligulata* A. Cunn. is a closely related, shrubby species, once regarded as a variety of *A. salicina*. It is widespread, usually occurring in dry, alkaline soils or coastal sand dunes. It flowers in profusion, with masses of orange-yellow **flower balls,** produced in August-September.

RIVER COOBA, EUMONG *A. stenophylla* A. Cunn. is somewhat similar to "Native Willow" but is usually more slender in growth. It inhabits inland watercourses often in association with "River Red Gum." The tree has very long, narrow, drooping **phyllodes,** up to 35 cm long, and is a particularly ornamental tree when seen at its best.

GOLDEN WREATH WATTLE, WILLOW WATTLE

Acacia saligna Wendl. LEGUMINOSAE

"Golden Wreath Wattle" is an extensively cultivated small, bushy tree noted for its rapidity of growth. Under favourable conditions it can reach tree size, **5–8 m high,** in 4–5 years after planting out as a small seedling.

The tree is native to Western Australia where it is often encountered along roadsides and elsewhere, in areas of at least moderate rainfall (400–800 mm annually). It has quite an extensive habitat range in the south-west, being found throughout the wheatlands and also in the Darling Range and "Jarrah" country, often where its roots are close to water.

There is a certain amount of confusion over the naming of this tree, some authorities listing it as the same species as "Orange Wattle" (*A. cyanophylla* Lindl.), another Western Australian small tree or large shrub, which has no apparent differences. Whether it is a separate species or not, there are two distinct forms of "Golden Wreath Wattle" in cultivation, one upright and slender, with an umbrageous crown, the other dense and low growing, usually with a thick, leaning **trunk** and rather heavy pendulous **branches** drooping to near the ground. **Bark** is rough, furrowed, and dark brown, but smooth and green on the small **branchlets. Phyllodes** are long, narrow, and ribbony, with a prominent midrib, and a dull dark green or blue-green in colour.

During October the tree is loaded down with axillary racemes of very large, globular yellow **flower heads** which make a spectacular show. The seeds germinate very freely and young plants can often be found under mature trees in their hundreds.

"Golden Wreath wattle" is a particularly hardy tree, growing equally well on most soil types and in areas where rainfall varies from as low as 250–1000 mm annually. It is an excellent tree as a quick shelter or to screen an ugly view in the garden, but cannot be considered permanent, as its life span is usually only 12–20 years. Sometimes the life span is prolonged in dry situations where growth is slower.

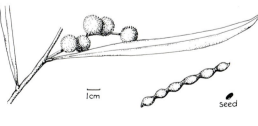

WESTERN MYALL

Acacia papyrocarpa Benth.
(syn. *A. sowdenii* Maiden). LEGUMINOSAE

"Western Myall" is a small tree of the low rainfall areas, extending from an eastern limit of the Flinders Ranges in South Australia to Balladonia in Western Australia. In certain parts, such as the countryside near Whyalla and Port Augusta in South Australia, it is the dominant tree of the area, and lends its own tough character to the countryside. Rainfall is 150–300 mm annually, and soils usually very alkaline, or limy.

The tree is only **5–8 m high,** with a dense, rounded crown, often broader than it is high. Sheep are fond of the foliage, and often nibble it off as high as they can reach, giving the tree a neatly trimmed, umbrageous appearance.

Phyllodes are long and narrow with a curved point; they are a silvery grey in colour, and the young tips are silky. This silvery foliage ripples and shines in the sun and wind, and is very lovely. The **bark** is dark, almost black, and very rough. Flowering is spasmodic, but in a good year the trees come alive with masses of small, deep-yellow **flower balls.**

The dark brown **timber** is dense and hard, and sometimes used to make ornamental woodwork boxes for cigars and jewels.

"Western Myall" is a distinctive, long-lived tree, particularly suited to harsh conditions where few trees are able to survive. This tree has no recovery from fire and can be completely wiped out in areas of bushfire.

A. loderi Maid. found near Broken Hill is very similar.

DROOPING MYALL *A. pendula* A. Cunn. is another lovely long-lived tree from the dry western plains of New South Wales, inland Queensland, and north-west Victoria. It is larger than "Western Myall," **up to 14 m high,** with rough **bark,** broader, knife-shaped (cultrate) **phyllodes,** and less conspicuous **flowers.**

It has beautiful drooping foliage. The thin, well-clothed, smaller **branches** hang vertically downwards, producing a lovely effect.

"Drooping Myall" prefers alluvial or heavy clay soils, its presence being considered a sign of good land. It is an excellent fodder tree, and is also a favourite meal of the bagmoth caterpillar which has seriously affected large areas of "Drooping Myall" country.

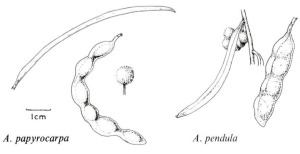

A. papyrocarpa   *A. pendula*

WESTERN AUSTRALIAN WILLOW MYRTLE
Agonis flexuosa Schau. MYRTACEAE

The "Western Australian Willow Myrtle" is a small tree prevalent throughout the wetter "Jarrah" and "Karri" forest country of southwestern Western Australia, including the Swan Coastal Plain where Perth is situated. The tree usually inhabits moist sandy soils, and is sometimes found in swamps.

It seldom exceeds **10–15 m in height.** When young it is a slender, drooping, single-stemmed tree that eventually produces a more spreading umbrageous crown of drooping willow-like habit. The **trunk** and **branches** are grey or dark brown with rough, furrowed **bark.** The tree lives to a great age when the trunk often becomes very thick and gnarled, with only a few upper branches. The **leaves** are quite broad and shining in the early stages with bronzy red new growth, but eventually revert to dark green; they are narrow and willowy with a pleasantly aromatic myrtle scent.

Flowers are small and white, but numerous, and clothe the hanging branches so that they appear to be covered with tiny white stars during spring months.

This tree is widely cultivated as a specimen tree, often used in place of the common "Weeping Willow" (*Salix*) which has such a voracious root system as to render it undesirable in small suburban gardens. It is very adaptable and will grow on most soils including sands and silts in seaside areas.

All the *Agonis* species found in Australia are native to the southwest of Western Australia, of which most are only of shrub size.

Agonis juniperina Schau. is one that can reach small tree proportions of usually only **about 7 m.** It is a slender, **rough-barked** tree of juniper-like foliage with very tiny **leaves** and small white star **flowers** in spring, but unlike the "Western Australian Willow Myrtle" in general appearance.

It is quite ornamental and easy to cultivate.

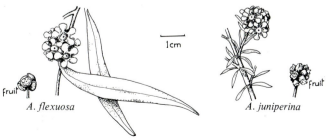

A. flexuosa   *A. juniperina*

ROUGH-BARKED APPLE

Angophora floribunda Sweet   MYRTACEAE
(syn. *A. intermedia* DC.).

Often mistaken for Eucalyptus trees, which they closely resemble in general appearance, particularly the "Bloodwood" group, angophoras are principally inhabitants of the wetter parts of New South Wales and Queensland.

"Rough-barked Apple" is widespread along the east coast from southern Queensland to north-west Victoria. In New South Wales it is also found scattered throughout the mountainous areas under 1200 m, and extending to the beginning of the dry western plains. The best climate for it is sub-tropical to temperate, with rainfall 500–1000 mm and alluvial or deep sandy loam soils.

It is a rather **short-trunked,** wide-spreading tree **14–24 m high,** with gnarled **branches** in older specimens. **Bark** is brown, persistent to the smaller branches, thick and fibrous.

The genus is mainly distinguished from *Eucalyptus* by the undeveloped flowers which have no operculum, or cap. The **fruits,** too, are ribbed, thin, and rather papery or fragile. Trees are free flowering with showy panicles of cream **flowers** prominently displayed in summer.

Eucalyptus **leaves** are usually but not always, alternate and scattered, whereas those of all species of *Angophora* are in opposite pairs. The leaves of this fine tree are bright green and show up conspicuously among other associated trees in forest stands.

"Rough-barked Apple" is an adaptable tree, useful for shade, shelter, and ornament.

There are six other species of *Angophora*, the best known being:

BROAD-LEAVED APPLE *A. subvelutina* F. Muell. A very similar **rough-barked** tree, but easily distinguished by its stalkless **leaves** which are heart-shaped at the base. **SMOOTH-BARKED APPLE** *A. costata* Domin (syn. *A. lanceolata* Cav.) Similar in size and habit but with a smooth **bark** that is shed annually leaving a smooth, dimpled pale orange or pink surface which ages to a grey colour. This tree is common in the Sydney-Newcastle sandstone areas, and is sometimes called "Sydney Apple." It is more prevalent, however, in Queensland where it enjoys an extensive range.

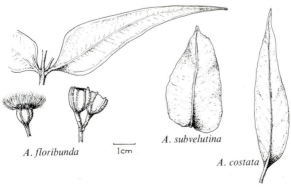

A. floribunda   1cm   *A. subvelutina*   *A. costata*

BUNYA PINE

Araucaria bidwillii Hook. ARAUCARIACEAE

"Bunya Pine" belongs to the group of well-known tropical softwood trees known as "Kauri Pine." This group consists of *Agathis robusta* F. M. Bail., "Queensland Kauri Pine," *Araucaria cunninghamii* Ait. ex D. Don, "Hoop Pine," and the "Bunya Pine." These are all fine timber trees native to the rain forests of eastern Australia, mainly Queensland, the "Hoop Pine" extending to New Guinea. They are often a feature of the skyline, towering over other species in the rain forests where they occur.

"Bunya Pine" has a very restricted natural distribution, and is only found in Queensland between Gympie and the Bunya Mountains, with an isolated occurrence much further north near Port Douglas. The tree favours rich volcanic soils preferably in moist valleys and low elevations. Rainfall is 370–1250 mm mainly in summer. It always occurs as a scattered tree dominating other species in the area. It is a particularly striking tree growing **to 50 m** with a large symmetrical dome-shaped crown like an elongated beehive.

The 60–120 cm diameter **trunk** is a long, straight, cylindrical bole, tapering only slightly to the top of the tree. The **branches** which radiate from the trunk are almost horizontal, but with a slight downward trend. They converge closer together near the top of the tree. The dark grey **bark** is hard and rough over the trunk and branches and is cracked into thin, horizontal scales. The crowded, hard, dark green **leaves** are flat and glossy, and spiral from the branchlets.

The **male flowers** which are long thin spikes at the ends of the branchlets appear in Sept.–Oct. on the same tree as the **female flowers.** These arise laterally from the branchlets and are composed of crowded carpels which develop into fruiting cones. These cones are pineapple-shaped, large and woody, up to 30 cm long by about 20 cm in diameter. They contain large **seeds** with a milky flesh and were once relished by the Aborigines.

"Bunya Pine" yields a **timber** similar to the other "Kauri Pines," all of which are prominent Australian softwoods.

Although too large for average gardens, it is occasionally planted as a park tree and grows successfully as far south as Adelaide provided there is adequate moisture.

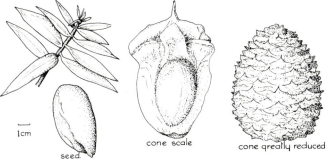

seed

cone scale

cone greatly reduced

1cm

TULIP OAK, BLACK JACK

Argyrodendron actinophyllum H. L. Edlin. STERCULIACEAE

One of the commonest trees of the mountainous rain forest scrubs of southern Queensland, particularly the Macpherson Range, "Tulip Oak" is also found as far south as Gloucester in New South Wales.

It is a tall, erect, stately tree of up **to 50 m in height** with a dense, glossy, handsome foliage. The **trunk,** usually about 1 m in diameter, has prominent, rather broad buttressing. **Bark** is dark brown, finely fissured, and shed in rather small flaky pieces. The very attractive compound **leaves** on long stalks are alternate, and consist of leaflets radiating from the top of the stalk in umbrella-like fashion. Although not as large or as thick and leathery, they are otherwise very similar to the leaves of the "Umbrella Tree" (*Schefflera actinophylla*, p. 212). The small white **flowers** have no petals, are bell-shaped, and appear in long axillary panicles during April. **Fruit** is a carpel, 4–6 cm long, containing a rounded **seed** at the base with a flat, thin wing near the top of the carpel.

There is only one other known species of *Argyrodendron* in Australia, although that particular species has a number of varieties mainly found in the tropical north of Queensland near Cairns and Atherton.

CROWSFOOT ELM *A. trifoliatum* F. Muell. is similar in size and habit to "Tulip Oak." It is very common throughout the coastal scrubs, particularly of Queensland, but also northern New South Wales. The thin-sectioned, web-like buttressing of this tree is a distinctive feature, and quite different from that of "Tulip Oak." It is easily recognised by its **leaves** which consist of 3 leaflets 7–12 cm long, at the ends of long stalks. The underside of the **leaves, flowers,** and **branchlets** are covered with small, silvery, or coppery scales.

Timber of both species is tough and straight grained; it has many uses, but must be treated against borer attack.

Both trees can be successfully grown as far south as Adelaide in deep soils with assured water, but eventually they will grow too large for the average-sized gardens.

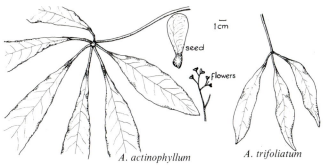

A. actinophyllum   *A. trifoliatum*

KING WILLIAM PINE
Athrotaxis selaginoides D. Don. TAXODIACEAE

Native to the cool rain forests of south-west Tasmania, mature specimens of "King William Pine" are no longer common, owing to the demand for its very valuable softwood timber.

The genus is limited to two species only, these being the only representatives of Taxodiaceae in the southern hemisphere. This family includes the mighty sequoias or "Redwoods" of North America, of which *S. sempervirens* is the world's tallest tree.

"King William Pine" grows in a cool temperate climate with a rainfall of 1500–2500 mm annually, and with snow quite common in winter.

At its best it **seldom reaches 35 m in height;** it has a sparse crown of foliage, and often a forked **trunk** sometimes buttressed at the base. **Bark** is reddish-brown, persistent throughout, with a soft spongy texture, longitudinally furrowed. The spirally arranged, small, crowded **leaves** are keeled and sharply pointed. Male and female **flowers** occur on the same tree, terminal fruiting cones being stalkless, and reaching maturity in one season.

Timber is a very durable, easily worked softwood with a pleasant cedar scent. It has many uses.

The tree is very slow growing and unknown in cultivation.

The other species, *A. cupressoides* D. Don. is quite rare.

There are two other famous Tasmanian pines confined mainly to the south-western half, both slow-growing, excellent timber trees that are now in only limited supply.

HUON PINE *Dacrydium franklinii* Hook. f. is found mainly in swampy or moist soils of the river flats. It is usually a shaft-like tree **under 35 m high,** with a slightly rough, persistent grey **bark,** and thick, keeled, closely imbricate **leaves. Fruiting cones** are minute near the ends of the branchlets. The **timber** contains a strongly scented resin that repels insects and makes it very durable as well as light and tough.

CELERY TOP PINE *Phyllocladus asplenifolius* Hook. f. is usually a **20–35 m** tree, sometimes dwarfed in exposed situations, with foliage consisting of broadly wedge-shaped, lobed cladodes (flattened branchlets), the true **leaves** appearing as tiny scales along the edges of the cladodes.

Athrotaxis selaginoides

Dacrydium franklinii

Phyllocladus aspleniifolius

GREY MANGROVE

Avicennia marina Vierh.　　　　　　　　　　　　VERBENACEAE

The "Mangroves" are an important feature of the vegetation in many parts of Australia. They grow along muddy sea-shores and tidal estuaries, and are usually found in dense stands known as "Mangrove swamps." These areas consist of salty, waterlogged mud which is frequently flooded by sea water and is intolerable to most plant life. These swamps act as a natural barrier protecting other plants from the sea water and salt winds.

The area beneath the "Mangrove" trees is often covered with a tangled jungle of long, arching roots which anchor the trees to the mud. As the root system develops, new growing shoots emerge which eventually form trees, and which in their turn repeat the process, thus producing a dense combination of enjoined trees. Under the trees peg-like, erect, aerial roots are also projected up through the mud; they absorb air at low tide. In this feature, *Avicennia* differs from *Rhizophora*, another genus of "Mangrove" from tropical Australia, which sends down aerial roots from the branches to stay them to the muddy soil beneath.

"Grey Mangrove" is usually a stout, crooked, low-branching tree less than **7 m in height,** and, in general shape, not unlike many banksia trees. Sometimes it grows to 14 m in height, but this is rare. The light grey **bark** is smooth and thin. The **leaves** are in opposite pairs, thick and broadly lanceolate, about 7·5 cm long, and bright glossy green with a white, silky undersurface. The tiny, orange, sessile **flowers** are on rigid stalks in axillary clusters, and much loved by bees. They usually occur in summer. "Mangrove" **honey** has a distinctive and pleasing flavour. **Fruits** consist of a small 2-valved capsule containing one **seed** which germinates before dropping, usually vertically, in the mud. The **timber** is used in boat building.

The several other species of "Mangrove" in Australia belong to different genera, and are usually found in the sub-tropical or tropical areas. *Avicennia officinalis L.*, a closely related species, is now considered native to India, China, and the near East, but not to Australia.

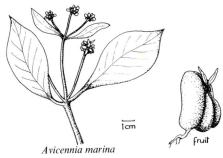

Avicennia marina

fruit

GIANT BANKSIA

Banksia grandis Willd.   PROTEACEAE

"Giant Banksia," so named because of its giant flower spikes and leaves, both often over 30 cm in length, is perhaps the most commonly encountered of all the western banksia trees. It is found from some 320 km north of Perth, to the lateritic gravelly soils of the Darling Range as an understorey tree to eucalypt forest, and extends throughout the "Jarrah" and "Karri" forests (sometimes with its base totally immersed in water during winter), to the south coast near Albany. Here it appears with "Jarrah" in a stunted form on rocky granite slopes or limestone cliffs.

The genus *Banksia* commemorates the name of Sir Joseph Banks and is entirely Australian. Of approximately sixty species now recorded, about fifty are native to Western Australia. With few exceptions these inhabit poor sandy or gravelly soils either in forest, woodland, or inland sand heath. The majority do not reach tree size and are usually large bushy shrubs, but sometimes only small, even prostrate dwarfs. Their usual flowering period is late summer through autumn and winter, when flowers are scarce, although some are spring flowering.

"Giant Banksia" is only a small tree seldom exceeding about **8 m in height.** In its young stages it grows very straight and upright, and with its large, deeply saw-toothed **leaves** and handsome soft woolly reddish-coloured new growth, it rather resembles a tropical hothouse plant. Eventually it forms a tree of fairly upright shape with rough grey **bark,** and sometimes with spreading **limbs.** The huge divided **leaves,** with a silvery reverse, form a circlet around the **flower spikes** which emerge in spring and summer, like large erect golden candles. These are followed by long **fruiting cones** with sharp **seed follicles.**

This tree is particularly ornamental, and can be grown in dense shade as well as in other conditions. Few of the western banksias, however, have yet proved reliable in cultivation, although the unique beauty of this lovely genus warrants every effort by the horticulturalist to tame it for garden culture.

Photograph by courtesy of G. D. Watton

fruit

1cm

HOLLY-LEAVED BANKSIA
Banksia ilicifolia R.Br. PROTEACEAE

"Holly-leaved Banksia" differs from most of the *Banksia* group in so far as the flowers form a rounded rosette encircled by the leaves, rather than the usual flowering spike.

The characteristic **inflorescences** of the genus are large, dense cylindrical spikes, sometimes up to more than 30 cm long and 7 cm or more in diameter, and usually sit upright on the branches. These spikes which contain many individual flowers form thick woody **fruiting cones**, each fruit (or follicle) in the cone containing two valves in which are two black, winged **seeds**. The fruits only open after extreme heat, and must be exposed to a flame, or allowed to remain in a hot oven for some time in order to extract the seeds.

Banksia trees are rather crooked, with a bushy crown, and a stout, gnarled **stem** covered with thick grey **bark**, and seldom exceed **10 m in height**. Main differences are in the leaves which are often large and deeply serrated, and, in some cases, in the inflorescences.

"Holly-leaved Banksia" is usually a stiff tree of the above description, although it occurs in several different forms. It was common in the Perth metropolitan area where it grows into an erect, narrow tree, and is distributed throughout the sandy coastal plains from about Mt Lesueur to Albany and the Stirling Range in the south. The **leaves** are dense and glossy and form a wreathlike effect around the terminal rounded spikes which can be red or yellow. It flowers from August to November.

Other tree banksias found in Western Australia include **FIRE-WOOD BANKSIA**, *B. menziesii* R.Br. and **ORANGE BANKSIA**, *B. prionotes* Lindl., which are gnarled and crooked trees somewhat alike in appearance, and with large, handsome, acorn-chaped **flower spikes**. In the former, these are usually various shades of red or yellow; in the latter, they are a most striking orange and woolly grey, both appearing prominently above the long, toothed **leaves** in autumn. "Fire-wood Banksia" is a familiar tree in and near Perth, and has much the same habitat range in the south-west as "Orange Banksia," the latter extending further inland.

The beautiful red **WARATAH BANKSIA**, *B. coccinea* R.Br. from the Stirling Range and Albany district, sometimes reaches tree size, but is usually only a single-stemmed, spindly shrub.

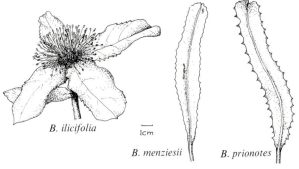

B. ilicifolia *B. menziesii* *B. prionotes*

COAST BANKSIA

Banksia integrifolia L.f.　　　　　　　　　　　PROTEACEAE

Of the eastern banksias "Coast Banksia" is perhaps the best-known tree; it is often found inhabiting coastal sites along the sandy shores of many parts of Victoria, New South Wales, and southern Queensland. It sometimes extends further inland, and is found in mountainous country, often in a stunted, shrubby form.

Usually **under 10 m,** the tree, particularly in coastal situations, is most often gnarled and crooked or straggling, buffeted by strong sea winds. The irregular shapes so formed display a character and harsh beauty often associated with hard conditions. The tree has a rough, light grey **bark,** and dark-green, smooth-edged **leaves** with a silvery reverse, which is particularly striking in windy weather. They are rounded at the tips and taper to a short stalk with a prominent midrib, 7–14 cm long by about 1 cm broad.

The pale yellow **inflorescences** are 6–12 cm long by about 5 cm in diameter, and occur in dense cylindrical spikes in autumn-winter.

The **timber** is soft and easily worked, and is occasionally used for small fancy woodwork.

"Coast Banksia" is an excellent tree for seaside conditions; it thrives in the acid, sandy soils of many parts of the eastern States, and is also a useful **honey** tree.

SILVER BANKSIA, *B. marginata* Cav. is a similar tree but of more regular shape, often well branched to near ground level. It is widely distributed in the eucalypt forest areas of the eastern States and extends to the wetter parts of South Australia such as the Mount Lofty Ranges and the South-East, and to Tasmania.

A very rewarding sight in mid-winter is this tree massed in **flowers** and **seed cones** and showing all the various flowering stages at the one time. When half-opened they are slender and greenish; at maturity they are pale yellow; then they darken with age, until the very old spikes become grey although they still retain their characteristic shape; and finally come the **fruiting cones.**

This is a lovely tree, well worth cultivating, but it prefers adequate moisture, good drainage, and acid soils.

The remaining eastern banksias are mainly large shrubby species, although the common **SAW BANKSIA,** *B. serrata* L.f. reaches tree proportions under favourable conditions.

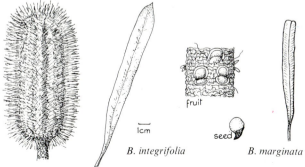

fruit

seed

B. integrifolia   1cm   *B. marginata*

SWAMP BANKSIA

Banksia littoralis R.Br. PROTEACEAE

"Swamp Banksia" is a familiar small tree of the low-lying sandy swamps and depressions of the coastal plains of south-west Western Australia. Although recorded from the Hill River district north of Perth, it is mainly a tree which is found from near Perth to Albany in the south.

The tree is usually of straggly habit and grows to **8 m or more in height**. It is **thick-trunked**, with a spreading, slightly drooping canopy of **branches**. The **bark** is rough and dull grey, but grey-tomentose on the younger branchlets. Although variable, the long linear soft **leaves** are typically 8–30 cm long by 4–6 mm wide, scattered, or irregularly whorled along the branches, and serrated with a few small soft teeth, usually more frequent near the apex. Their undersurface is hoary or felted white. The **inflorescences** occur as erect, cylindrical spikes produced in the forks between branchlets, at first a burnished gold, but turning yellow as the individual flowers open. **Flowers** occur from late summer to winter. The **fruiting cones** which follow subtend many flat, sharp, and protruding seed capsules.

RIVER BANKSIA, *B. littoralis* R.Br. var. *seminuda* A.S. George, is found along river banks and wet depressions from Banksiadale to the Albany area. This forms an erect, shapely, and extremely handsome tree which grows to **25 m high** at its best, with fresh green luxuriant **leaves**. These are arranged in whorls along the branches in similar manner to the leaves of the shrubby *Banksia verticillata* from granite outcrops near Albany.

COAST BANKSIA, *B. attenuata* R.Br., is another western tree *Banksia* mainly of the coastal districts of south-west Western Australia. It is usually a small bushy tree with long narrow **leaves** which are gently and evenly serrated and taper to the base. The terminally erect, slender **flower spikes** are an intense sulphur yellow.

All three trees prefer sandy or loamy acid soils where an abundance of water is available.

Photograph of Banksia attenuata

1cm *B. littoralis* *B. verticillata* (fruit) *B. attenuata*

FLAME TREE, ILLAWARRA FLAME TREE
Brachychiton acerifolium F. Muell. STERCULIACEAE

At its best, "Flame Tree" is one of Australia's most beautiful flowering trees, and is extensively cultivated in Australia and overseas for ornamentation. It is an inhabitant of the sub-tropical brush forests from the Illawarra district in New South Wales to near Innisfail in Queensland.

Brachychiton are mainly trees of the tropics where it is their habit to deciduate or partly deciduate following the "Dry" (winter), flower, and produce new foliage when the summer "Wet" begins. When planted in temperate climates of mainly winter rain, they retain this characteristic and still drop their leaves in late spring, prior to early summer flowering. They are typically pyramidal trees with a trunk which tapers from the base to a slender tip. Their seed is hairy or bristly and contained in large boat-shaped follicles. When shed, the seed leaves an outer coat which forms a honeycomb structure within the follicles. The generic name is derived from this, "Brachy" meaning short, and "Chiton" a coat, referring to this loose outer covering of the seed.

"Flame Tree" is naturally a large pyramidal tree **to 40 m high,** although it never attains this size when cultivated in the south. The large palmate **leaves** are glossy and variable, often deeply divided into 5–7 lobes. The brilliant-scarlet, waxy bell **flowers** on scarlet stalks appear in November or December in numerous axillary clusters. In a good year these cover the whole tree after leaf fall, producing a glorious effect. The bristly **seeds** are bright yellow and contained in follicles up to 10 cm long. "Flame Tree" is cultivated successfully as far south as Adelaide, but prefers fairly rich, moist, non-calcareous soils.

LACEBARK TREE, WHITE KURRAJONG *B. discolor* F. Muell. is a closely related tree common in cultivation, and native to the brush forests of Queensland, mainly, but also of northern New South Wales. Its deep-pink, hairy **flowers** are large and conspicuous, and make a fine display in early summer when the tree partly deciduates.

Brachychiton hybridize very freely, several hybrids of the above species being in cultivation. One known as *B. hybrida* is a particularly fine specimen tree.

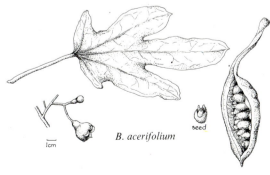

B. acerifolium

KURRAJONG

Brachychiton populneum R.Br. STERCULIACEAE

"Kurrajong" is a commonly cultivated versatile tree which is naturally widely distributed in eastern Australia. It occurs from inland and southern Queensland throughout New South Wales, but particularly on the western slopes and plains, and in east and north-east Victoria. The tree is found on a variety of soils, but often shows preference for those of limestone origin.

The name "Kurrajong" originated from an Aboriginal word "currajong" meaning "fibre-yielding plant," the bark fibres being used by Aborigines for making nets.

The tree is densely foliaged, and of moderate to large size, **usually 14–20 m high,** with a stout, grey-barked **trunk.** In its early stages it grows pyramidal with a green **bark,** but in time it develops a spreading crown which gives dense shade. The glossy dark-green **leaves** occur on long stalks (petioles), and are very variable in shape, from entire and poplar-like, to partly divided or deeply lobed. When young they are pale green, almost chartreuse in colour, the whole tree having this appearance when producing its new foliage.

The small bell-shaped **flowers** borne in axillary panicles are cream or greenish, with red, yellow, or purplish-coloured throats. The seed follicles are about 8 cm long, and the **seeds** black and numerous. Flowering is variable, usually March to early summer.

"Kurrajong" is an extremely valuable tree, adaptable to soils, deep rooted, and excellent for ornament, shade, and shelter, as well as a good fodder tree in times of drought. Its virtues are appreciated by landowners who now preserve it, particularly in the drier areas of its range.

DESERT KURRAJONG *B. gregorii* F. Muell. is a smaller dry area species belonging to the same group and superficially often resembling a poor specimen of "Kurrajong." The **leaves** are composed of 3–5 linear-lanceolate lobes, and the seed follicles are smaller than those of the "Kurrajong," with fewer **seeds** in each. **Flowers** are pale yellow. This tree is found in arid parts from the Murchison River in Western Australia to north of Kalgoorlie, thence across the Victoria Desert to the region of the Musgrave, Birksgate, and Mann Ranges in South and Western Australia.

Leaf variations
B. populneum
seed
1cm

NATIVE BOX, SWEET BURSARIA, CHRISTMAS BUSH

Bursaria spinosa Cav.　　　　　　　　　　PITTOSPORACEAE

"Native Box" is a widespread species found throughout temperate Australia. It occurs on many different soil types and environments, often as quite a small shrub to only about **2 m high,** but in other situations as a small, rather spreading tree **to 7–10 m high.** In the South-East of South Australia it forms quite a handsome tree, particularly along the coast.

The common name of "Native Box" was originated by the early settlers because of the resemblance of the leaves to the common English "Box Tree."

The tree is only **short-trunked,** often crooked, with a very rugged dark-grey **bark** and small thorns or spines on the **branchlets.** The **leaves** are scattered and very variable, entire, and usually obovate or ovate-lanceolate in shape. They are bright glabrous green on both sides with a prominent midrib.

About Christmastime and later, the plant flowers, producing an abundance of small, sweetly scented, white or cream, star-shaped **blossoms.** These are borne above the foliage on dense, upright panicles which make a fine show, and attract bees in large swarms.

The small, brown purse-like or pouched **seed vessels** that follow give to the plant its generic name of *Bursaria*, meaning pouch-like capsules.

"Native Box" is seldom seen in cultivation, but should receive more attention as an ornamental small-flowering tree or shrub. It will grow in most soils and situations but is more likely to reach tree size where moisture is abundant. When kept to shrubby proportions it makes quite an attractive and useful hedge plant.

There are only three Australian species of *Bursaria*.

BOX OLIVE WOOD *B. incana* Lindl. is a small, erect tree from southern Queensland with small **leaves** which are hoary underneath, and terminal panicles of white **flowers.**

B. spinosa

1cm

WHITE BOTTLE-BRUSH
Callistemon salignus DC.　　　　　　　　　　　　　　MYRTACEAE

"White Bottle-brush" is **only a small tree,** sometimes a shrub, which is widely distributed throughout temperate Australia in forest country extending from Queensland as far north as Bundaberg to the Torrens Gorge near Adelaide in South Australia. Different forms of the same species can be found within this range.

This is a tree member of the well-known "Bottle-brush" group consisting mainly of large shrubs which are commonly cultivated both in Australia and overseas, and prized for the beauty of their large, spectacular flowers.

Callistemons are characterized by these conspicuous and stalkless (sessile) **flowers** which consist of numerous long stamens, usually a vivid red, but sometimes cream, greenish-yellow, or pink. The flower filaments are separated or free, and distinguished from the genus *Melaleuca* whose filaments are joined or united in bundles. The dense flower heads are prolific in spring, and are sometimes followed by a lesser flowering about autumn.

The flowers are followed by hard, woody **seed capsules** which encircle the stem in a close cylindrical group, and take about 3 years to mature. The minute seeds remain viable for many years until fire or some other means allows the fruits to open.

"White Bottle-brush" is usually a bushy crowned tree up to **10 m in height. The trunk** is slender with a whitish papery **bark.** The narrow, pointed **leaves** are shining and willowy, 5–10 cm long by about 1 cm broad, with a distinct midrib, their most striking feature being the bright pink to red colour of the new growing tips. This is soft and downy and makes a display as attractive as the flowers.

The **flowers** are usually a creamy-white colour, although pink and red colour forms occur. **Fruits** are rounded, about 3 mm in diameter.

This is a useful tree for beekeepers as it helps to build up **nectar** and pollen supplies in the spring for bee colonies. Being adaptable it is also valued as an ornamental tree, although it prefers non-limestone moist soils. It flowers at the same time as the "Weeping Bottle-brush" (see p. 56), and planted together, the two make a spectacular display of red and white blossom.

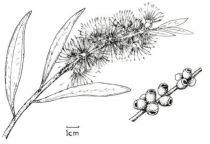

WEEPING BOTTLE-BRUSH
Callistemon viminalis G. Don ex Loud. MYRTACEAE

"Weeping Bottle-brush" is a commonly cultivated tree naturally found growing mainly along the banks of rivers and creeks throughout eastern Queensland and north-eastern New South Wales north of the Hunter River. In some parts it extends into the higher tablelands.

This tree is the largest member of the "Bottle-brush" family, sometimes reaching **20 m in height,** although usually under **10 m.** The common name, "Bottle-brush" is reserved for members of the *Callistemon* genus, although several other Australian plants such as some *Melaleuca* and *Banksia* species also have flowers of this shape.

The "Weeping Bottle-brush" is often scraggy when seen growing naturally, but usually forms a neat, willowy tree with long, slender and drooping smaller **branches** when cultivated. The **trunk** is slender, and the **bark** rough, dark grey, and furrowed. The long narrow **leaves** (about 7 cm long by 6 mm broad) have a prominent midrib, and are tapered at each end on very short stalks. When crushed they emit a pleasant myrtle scent.

The colour of the leaves varies as they age. The very new tips are a bright, bronzy red, and are soft and downy in texture. As they develop they change to a soft pale green and eventually mature to a more rigid darker green, the whole effect being very attractive.

The **flowers** appear in spring in dense red spikes that cover the whole tree in a blaze of colour. Irregular flowers occur at other times of the year also. They are variable in both size and form. Good flowering forms should be reproduced by cuttings which strike quite readily, rather than by seedlings which are often disappointing.

The hard, woody **fruits** are cup-shaped, about 5 mm by 5 mm. This tree is also a valuable producer of **nectar** and pollen for bee colonies. It is valued as an ornamental tree and is easily grown, preferring non-limestone soils with adequate moisture supplies. Under these conditions growth is quite rapid. It is also useful as a street tree where rainfall exceeds 400 mm annually.

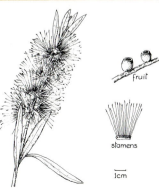

fruit

stamens

1cm

WHITE CYPRESS PINE
Callitris columellaris F. Muell.   CUPRESSACEAE

The *Callitris* or "Native Cypress Pines" are an ornamental and important group of conifers found throughout Australia, very often forming pure stands in moderately dry localities, particularly where there are sandy soils.

Several previously known species have now all been grouped under the one name of *C. columellaris*. This is a particularly widespread species and is found in all mainland States, though mainly on the east coast and the western plains and slopes of New South Wales, and in south-east Queensland. In South Australia it is prevalent in the scenic Flinders Ranges where it is sometimes the dominant tree on rocky slopes and rises, and enhances the landscape.

"White Cypress Pine" favours a warm, temperate inland climate with rainfall in the 400–750 mm range, although this is considerably higher in parts of the east coast, where climate is sub-tropical. It sometimes forms pure forests, but more often mixes with eucalyptus species, usually on sandy or loamy soils.

The genus is distinguished by the tiny scale-like **leaves** in whorls of 3 or 4 along the **branchlets,** and by the **fruiting cones** with six woody scales, three being distinctly smaller than the others. These contain hard, winged **seeds** which germinate very freely.

This particular species is a large, fastigiate tree, **20–30 m high** at its best, but is considerably smaller in some of its habitat localities. The **bark** is dark grey, rough, and furrowed, and persists to the smaller branches; the foliage is often glaucous. The **flowers** are not conspicuous, but appear as unisexual catkins. **Fruits** are dark brown and spherical, about 2 cm or less in diameter.

The softwood **timber** of this tree is renowned for its resistance to termite attack and is used extensively in the building trade.

There are several other species of native cypress pines, many of them visually alike. They are all ornamental, particularly when grown in clumps of 3 or 4 together, and should be more widely grown as garden trees.

fruit seed

1cm

NATIVE or WILD ORANGE

Capparis mitchellii Lindl.   CAPPARIDACEAE

Commemorating its discoverer, Sir Thomas Mitchell, "Native Orange" is only a small tree from the arid Inland. It is found in the far north of South Australia, mainly in the Cooper's Creek–Lake Frome area, in central Australia, and in the dry parts of New South Wales, Queensland, and Victoria, usually on clay or loamy soils. It is protected by law in South Australia.

In its early stages the plant is only a scrambly, prickly shrub, but soon develops to a more sturdy habit, and eventually forms a rather compact tree, often with several joined main stems. It is not a plant to go unnoticed because of its dense habit, and deep, sombre, green foliage, giving it a solid, permanent appearance as though it could withstand any adverse condition it might have to endure.

The **branches** of this small and compact tree, which grows **to about 7–8 m,** sometimes reach to near the ground. Often it is wider in girth than it is high. **Leaves** are broadly lance-shaped or ovate, about 5 cm long, and rather rough in texture, being clothed with a short, dense tomentum. The **flowers,** up to 6 cm across, are white or cream in colour, showy, and produced freely from September to November, though each flower only lasts one day. The flower consists of a bunch of about 50 long stamens in the centre of several rather broad petals. The solitary **fruit,** produced on long stems, is about the size of a golf ball. It is deep green, hard, and woody, and contains large flat **seeds.** At one time they were occasionally eaten by the Aborigines, but are not generally considered edible.

"Native Orange" is a very useful tree in the interior in that it provides shade and shelter for stock. It has been successfully cultivated in Adelaide and warrants consideration for garden culture, particularly in dry areas.

Capparis is a large genus of plants found in warm climates throughout the world. There are a number of other Australian species but these are shrubs or climbing plants, mostly native to Queensland.

BLACK BEAN, MORETON BAY CHESTNUT

Castanospermum australe A. Cunn.　　　　　LEGUMINOSAE

"Black Bean" is a tree of the brush forests of northern New South Wales and Queensland, where it extends as far north as Cape York Peninsula and inland some 150 km from the coast. It favours good, rich, moist soils following watercourses.

The tree is an ornamental one, as well as a much sought-after timber tree. In its natural environment it can reach a **height of 40 m,** but under cultivation, particularly in the cooler southern temperate locations such as Adelaide and Melbourne where it is successfully cultivated, it seldom exceeds 8–14 m. Here it sometimes forms a dense shade tree with several main stems.

Bark is slightly rough, grey or brown in colour, and the foliage dark green and glossy, and handsome at all times. **Leaves** are long (up to 50 cm) and divided into a number of leaflets (pinnate) of frond-like appearance. Each leaf consists of 8–17 alternate leaflets, 5–12 cm long, and narrow, elliptical, or oval in shape.

The **flowers,** which bloom in October–November on the previous season's wood, are pea-like, individually large (up to 4 cm long), and appear in showy racemes, usually a deep golden-orange in colour. The flowers are sometimes sparse, and in any case can be partly hidden by the dense foliage.

The **seeds** are contained in large, heavy brown **pods** up to 25 cm long, and are themselves large and brown, about the size of a large chestnut. When green they are poisonous to stock.

The attractive, dark-brown **timber** is hard and heavy, polishes and dresses well, and is prized for fancy woodwork and furniture of teak-like appearance.

"Black Bean" makes an excellent shade and shelter tree on cleared land and has sometimes been preserved for this purpose. It grows successfully in climates colder than in its natural environment, but should be grown on the moist, higher-grade soils of these areas.

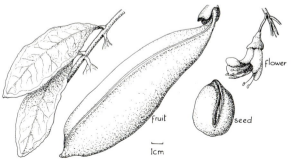

RIVER OAK

Casuarina cunninghamiana Miq. CASUARINACEAE

"River Oak" is the largest tree of the *Casuarina* family, a large and interesting group of Australian trees and shrubs known as "Oaks" or "Sheoaks," all of which possess certain peculiar characteristics.

These include long, needle-like, green cladodes which act as leaves but are really small branches. The true leaves are tiny teeth-like scales which encircle the joints of these cladodes at regular intervals. The male and female flowers occur on separate trees and appear in a different manner on each. On the female trees they are small, red-coloured, cone-shaped, and attached to the main branchlets by a short stalk; they are followed by woody cones containing the fruit. The male flowers appear as small terminal spikes at the ends of the cladodes; these are often a golden-brown or red in colour, and so abundant that they create a very beautiful effect.

"River Oak" is a natural inhabitant of freshwater rivers and streams of the relatively high rainfall country (500 to over 1500 mm) of New South Wales, Queensland, and extending to Arnhem Land as far as the Daly River. Over this range conditions vary from dry temperate, where frosts are quite severe, to tropical, where frosts are nil. At all times its need of water other than natural rainfall is apparent. Soils are usually alluvial loams or sands.

The tree is large, majestic, and pyramidal, **15–35 m high,** with an upright **trunk.** The **branches** are fairly densely clothed, horizontal to semi-pendulous, sometimes occurring near ground level; foliage is a lustrous green and pine-like. The **bark** on the trunk and main limbs is rough, deeply furrowed, and dark grey in colour.

"River Oak" is an ornamental species good for cultivation, adaptable to soil differences, and able to tolerate rainfall as low as 375 mm. It flowers from April to October.

SWAMP OAK *C. glauca* Sieb. Robust and erect, this is a somewhat similar but more sombre tree, native to the brackish lagoons and tidal rivers of east and south-east Australia. It is widely planted on account of its ability to flourish under harsh conditions on practically any soil including saline. It suckers freely and forms a good windbreak.

BULL OAK or **BULOKE,** *C. leuhmanni* R. T. Baker, a tall tree of very similar appearance to "Swamp Oak," is native to the moderately dry inland areas of eastern Australia.

C. cunninghamiana

C. glauca 1cm.

C. leuhmanni

DESERT OAK

Casuarina decaisneana F. Muell.   CASUARINACEAE

"Desert Oak" is perhaps the loveliest of all the "Sheoak" or casuarina trees. It is an inhabitant of the dry inland areas of central Australia where it is almost always found growing in the red sand dunes.

The tree itself varies in each stage of its growth. In its juvenile form it is fastigiate in habit, and rather tall and slender. As it matures it begins to develop a more dense habit, but it is not until it reaches full maturity that its characteristic shape is finally reached.

Usually a tree up to **10 m in height,** it occasionally grows higher. Its spread varies considerably, but the tree can be as broad as it is high. It has a graceful weeping habit, characteristic of the "Sheoak" group.

The foliage is usually a dull green that blends perfectly with the background colour of the red sand dunes, with which it is usually associated. Its straight **trunk** is dark brown, almost black, and very deeply furrowed.

The **seed cones** which are produced on the female trees are the largest of the genus, and are about 5 cm or more long and up to 4 cm in width. **Timber** is very strong and durable.

Little is known about "Desert Oak" as a cultivated tree, but its reluctance to grow anywhere but on deep sand would indicate that perfect drainage is required for its successful growth.

The sight of the "Desert Oak" on red sand dunes near Mount Olga and Ayers Rock, or backed by the blue Mann Ranges, is surely enough to inspire appreciation of one of the most striking trees of dry, inland Australia.

BELAH, BLACK OAK *C. cristata* Miq. is another dry area tree common in parts of South Australia, Victoria, and New South Wales. When seen in areas of very low rainfall and harsh conditions it is **usually a poor specimen 7–10 m high.** Where water is available, however, "Belah" grows to a fine tree to 20 m, suitable for farm or ornamental planting on most soils, and not unlike "Swamp Oak" (*C. glauca*) in general habit.

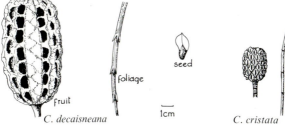

fruit — foliage — seed — *C. decaisneana* — 1cm — *C. cristata*

DROOPING SHEOAK, SHEOKE

Casuarina stricta Ait. CASUARINACEAE

"Drooping Sheoak" is a relatively small-growing tree inhabiting many parts of southern and eastern temperate Australia. It is found in New South Wales, Victoria, South Australia, and Tasmania.

The tree is often seen along the coast in calcareous sands which are subjected to a fierce buffeting by salt-laden winds. Further inland it occurs on poor rocky soils where it is often the dominant tree in areas with about 350 mm rainfall, but it is seen at its best in open forest country of moderate rainfall. Here soils are usually sand, often overlying a clay subsoil.

The tree has a single, erect **stem,** with rough, persistent, dark-grey **bark,** and a compact, bushy crown of pendulous foliage, which gives dense shade. The long, ribbed, needle-like **branches** are dark green, and droop significantly giving the tree its attractive and characteristic weeping appearance. **Usually only 5–8 m high, it sometimes reaches 14 m.**

Male specimens often flower profusely in late autumn, when they are smothered in small golden-brown or rust-coloured **flowers.** The effect is one of the loveliest produced by any Australian tree. When the flowers drop and cover the ground beneath the tree the effect is almost as lovely. **Fruiting cones** are dark grey, rather large (up to 5 cm long), and oval-shaped with prominent valves.

Adaptable to most soils and situations, "Drooping Sheoak" is a fine farm, shade, and shelter tree. It should also be cultivated more for ornament, particularly in difficult coastal sites and windy situations where the choice of trees is limited.

Although *C. stricta* is not recorded in Western Australian flora, another species, *C. acutivalvis* F. Muell. is so similar that it may be a variety.

WESTERN AUSTRALIAN SHEOAK *C. fraserana* Miq. is a very handsome species native to moist sandy soils in the south-west. It forms a lovely small tree with deep, lustrous green foliage and a smoother **trunk** than most trees of the genus.

 fruit *C. stricta*

 foliage

 male flowers

 seed 1cm

 C. fraserana

FOREST OAK, ROSE SHEOAK

Casuarina torulosa Ait. CASUARINACEAE

"Forest Oak" is a slender, pyramidal tree of the coastal eucalyptus forests of eastern Australia extending from Cairns in northern Queensland to as far south as Nowra in New South Wales.

Most of this habitat is sub-tropical to tropical in climate with mainly summer rainfall, although in its southern extremity, and on the tablelands in New South Wales frosts are not uncommon, and there is some snow at the higher altitudes.

Although found at sea level "Forest Oak" is more commonly encountered in hilly country usually on moist fertile soils, and mainly as a secondary species to forest eucalypts such as "Sydney Blue Gum" (*E. saligna*). Annual rainfall is 750–1250 mm.

Depending on conditions the tree varies from **10–25 m in height** with an erect, slender, rough **trunk,** and wispy, drooping, rather open foliage. The dark grey **bark** is rough and persistent on both trunk and main branches, closely furrowed down and across, and corky. The fine, wispy, needle-like **cladodes** sometimes appear in a pinkish colour, a very attractive feature of the tree from which it gets its common name, "Rose Sheoak." The woody cones enclosing the **fruits** are globular or barrel-shaped, about 1·5–2·5 cm in diameter.

Because of its habit and coloured foliage this is an extremely ornamental tree suited for planting in areas of assured rainfall. It does well as far south as South Australia in the cooler areas such as the Mount Lofty Ranges where it seldom grows any larger than a slender 8–12 m tree.

BLACK SHEOAK *C. suberosa* Otto et Dietr. (syn. *C. littoralis* Salisb.). This is an erect, sometimes conical, tree **to 14 m high** commonly found in the eastern States and Tasmania, particularly on poor sandstone soils. It forms a handsome specimen or shelter tree in areas of assured rainfall.

The **timber** of both trees is hard and durable, and can be given an ornamental appearance when used for veneers and joinery. In common with most casuarinas it burns with great heat and was once prized as fuel.

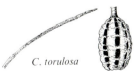

C. torulosa 1cm *C. suberosa* seed

COACHWOOD, SCENTED SATINWOOD
Ceratopetalum apetalum D. Don. CUNONIACEAE

"Coachwood" is one of the most important timber trees of the New South Wales coastal brush forests where it occurs from Bateman's Bay in the south to as far north as the Macpherson Range near the Queensland border.

The genus *Ceratopetalum* consists of five species, of which only one, *C. succirubrum*, is found away from the tropical or sub-tropical east coast of Australia. This species occurs also in New Guinea. They are characterised by the toothed leaves which are one to three foliate and opposite, and the four or five calyx segments with twice this number of stamens. **Fruits** are small and hard and surrounded by horizontal wing-like calyx lobes which turn bright red in some species.

"Coachwood" is a tall, shaft-like, forest tree **to 35 m high** and a **trunk** up to 1 m in diameter with a rough **bark.** The bark and wood are fragrant, owing apparently to the presence of the substance, coumarin. The **leaves** are usually solitary, lanceolate or elliptical, and up to 13 cm long. The **flowers** have no petals, but the calyx lobes enlarge and turn a bright reddish colour, giving the tree colour in early summer.

The pale pink **timber** is light, strong, and easily worked and used extensively for furniture and interior woodwork.

This is an ornamental tree for moist, sheltered situations.

NEW SOUTH WALES CHRISTMAS BUSH *C. gummiferum* Sm. is the species well known in cultivation. It is native to northern and central coastal New South Wales, usually on sandstone where it is **often only shrubby, but sometimes reaches tree proportions.** It is the only species with petals. These are small, jagged, and white, and soon fall, leaving numerous calyx lobes which swell and turn a bright red or pink about Christmastime when they make a spectacular display. The **leaves** are shining and 3-lobed.

This species is very ornamental, but not easy to cultivate, except in conditions akin to its natural environment.

The other three species, **DOGWOOD** *C. virchowii* F. Muell., *C. corymbosum* C. T. White, and *C. succirubrum* C. T. White are all tall **timber** trees found in the Atherton Tableland regions of northern Queensland.

C. apetalum   *C. gummiferum*

NATIVE POPLAR
Codonocarpus pyramidalis F. Muell. PHYTOLACCACEAE

A very attractive, upright tree endemic only to South Australia, "Native Poplar" is found in the northern part of the State, mainly in the northern Flinders Range area.

The genus, consisting of only three species, is confined to Australia.

"Native Poplar" is a slender, upright tree **to 8 m high,** with a light fawn or brownish-coloured, smooth **trunk,** and elegant, drooping **branches.** Where it grows it is an unusual and conspicuous feature of the vegetation, particularly when seen as isolated specimens in open, flat country. Foliage is bright green with **leaves** 5–10 cm long, very narrow, and rather soft and smooth in texture.

The **flowers** are fairly insignificant, but are followed by bell-shaped **fruits,** produced in dense clusters usually near the top of the tree. These are about 1 cm long, greenish-yellow in colour, and very decorative usually occurring in summer, but variable.

It is doubtful if this tree has ever been cultivated. If tamed, especially in dry areas, it could become a popular and handsome subject for garden use.

C. cotinifolius F. Muell. is a related species also known as "Native Poplar." This species is a slender, upright, and graceful tree **7–14 m in height,** inhabiting the dry areas of all mainland States. It is often seen in pure stands, one such stand being near Curtin Springs on the way to Ayers Rock in central Australia.

The **leaves** are broader than in the preceding species and a bluish-green in colour. The name "Horse-radish Tree" or sometimes "Mustard Tree" originated from the taste of these leaves. A medicinal product with a peculiar bitter taste comes from the **bark,** and the **timber,** although soft, is insect-resistant and useful.

The remaining species, *C. australis* Cunn. known as "Bell Fruit Tree" is a similar, handsome tree **to 8 m high,** but with bright green, willow-like **leaves.** It is native only to New South Wales and Queensland.

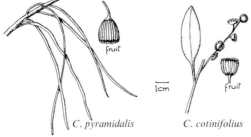

C. pyramidalis   *C. cotinifolius*

CUPANIA

Cupaniopsis anacardioides Radlk.   SAPINDACEAE

"Cupania" is a dense, evergreen tree native to the east coast of Australia from north of Sydney to Townsville in Queensland. It is very often found growing in coastal sands in isolated patches, and will withstand a certain amount of exposure to salt-laden winds, although too much exposure results in "burning off" on the windward side.

The tree resembles the cashew tree (*Anacardium*) from which it derives its specific epithet.

"Cupania" is not a tall tree, usually growing no higher than **8 m** but **sometimes reaching 14 m.** Its spread nearly always exceeds its height and this habit together with its dense foliage makes it an ideal shade or street tree. The **leaves** are pinnate, consisting of 2–12 leaflets, dark green and shining. The small greyish-white **flowers** occur in axillary or terminal panicles, but are insignificant. During November and December the numerous bright orange-red **fruits** of this tree can make a most attractive display. Unfortunately only a small percentage of "Cupania" possess this fruiting habit and the tree should be vegetatively propagated from good fruiting specimens.

This tree has received considerable attention as a street tree, particularly along the east coast, where it can be seen lining streets in towns from Newcastle to Rockhampton. Its wide-branching and low-growing habit make it ideal to plant beneath overhead service wires to provide dense shade on hot summer days. It is versatile as regards soils, and will withstand strong winds very well. "Cupania" is cultivated as far south as Adelaide in South Australia, where it forms a neat tree **to 8 m high.**

There are several other species of *Cupaniopsis* native to the east coast but they are not commonly encountered or cultivated.

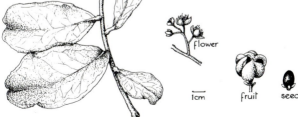

BLUE QUANDONG, BLUE FIG, BRACELET TREE
Elaeocarpus grandis F. Muell. ELAEOCARPACEAE

Native to the coastal brush forests of northern New South Wales to northern Queensland, "Blue Quandong" is a member of a large, mainly tropical genus of plants from the southern hemisphere. There are about twenty Australian species, all endemic. Several of these are large trees native only to tropical Australia, although one species, *E. reticulatus*, extends south as far as Tasmania.

The genus is distinguished by the smooth lobeless fruits (drupes) with a fleshy outer covering enclosing a hard stone.

"Blue Quandong" is a large tree over **33 m in height,** with a tall, strongly buttressed **trunk** supporting a slightly wrinkled, dark grey **bark.** The smooth **leaves** are thinly textured, with rather conspicuous veins and finely serrated margins, oblong-lanceolate in shape, 10–15 cm long by about 2·5 cm broad. As they age they change colour, until, just before they fall, they are an attractive bright red— at least in cooler, drier climates. The **flowers,** which resemble the "Lily of the Valley," are large and fringed, greenish-white in colour, and borne thickly in one-sided axillary racemes during spring. The bright blue "Quandong"-shaped **fruits** that follow are very decorative and give rise to the tree's common name. They enclose a hard, deeply wrinkled, 5-celled stone, the mature cells each containing a solitary, narrowly oval **seed.** These stones are sometimes used to make necklaces.

The useful **timber** is pale yellow, soft and light.

BLUEBERRY ASH *E. reticulatus* Smith (*E. cyaneus* Ait.). Sometimes called "Lily of the Valley Tree," this species is a much smaller, dense, bushy tree, but just as ornamental with similar **flowers** and elliptical-shaped blue **fruits.** It is widespread from Fraser Island off the Queensland coast throughout the east coast regions to Tasmania.

E. obovatus G. Don, also known as "Blueberry Ash," is a closely related larger tree that is found from near Sydney northwards to west of Bundaberg (Mount Perry) in Queensland.

Although rarely grown, these species are very decorative trees which are seldom too large for average gardens away from the tropics. They prefer moist, lime-free soils.

E. grandis

LONG-LEAVED EMU BUSH, BERRIGAN
Eremophila longifolia F. Muell. MYOPORACEAE

"Long-leaved Emu Bush" is a small tree member of a genus comprising mainly bushy shrubs with rather showy tubular flowers and usually favouring poor limestone soils in low rainfall areas of Australia. This particular species is found in all States in arid inland locations, often seen at its best along creek banks or sheltered gullies, and usually as single specimens. There are seldom more than two or three together.

The genus is purely Australian consisting of about eighty species. The name was derived from the Greek "Eremophiles," meaning desert loving. The fruits are a favourite food of the emu, and young seedlings of the bushes are sometimes obtained from emu droppings.

"Long-leaved Emu Bush" is usually a tree **to 7–8 m high** with many graceful, drooping **branches** and a slender **stem,** seldom reaching 30 cm in diameter. It often forms many root suckers. The rugged **bark** is brown and deeply fissured and resembles that of the "Sugarwood," *Myoporum platycarpum* (see p. 194), a tree with which it is often associated.

As its name implies, the dark olive-green **leaves** are long and drooping, up to 20 cm x 6 mm broad. They are very hairy when young, but at maturity are smooth, scattered, flat, and rather thick or fleshy. The tubular, often solitary **flowers** are pendulous, hairy, and deeply lobed at the mouth, usually a dull red or pink in colour, and spotted. They occur at various times throughout the year. The **fruits** are succulent egg-shaped drupes with a long slender style attached until maturity.

The **timber** is pale brown, hard, and close grained.

This tree is a useful shelter and fodder tree in arid parts, particularly on calcareous soils and could well be used for ornamental purposes in inland towns where the choice of a small shade tree is limited. It is protected by law in South Australia.

BUDDA *Eremophila mitchellii* Benth. is a species from the western plains of New South Wales which sometimes forms a small graceful tree. The **leaves** are much shorter than those of *E. longifolia* (2–7 cm) and the **flowers** fragrant, and purple or white in colour. The **timber** of this tree is white-ant resistant and useful for fence posts.

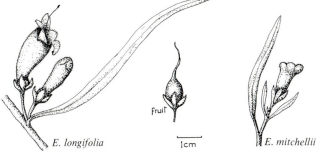

E. longifolia fruit 1cm *E. mitchellii*

BATS-WING CORAL TREE, BEAN TREE
Erythrina vespertilio Benth. LEGUMINOSAE

The "Coral Trees" belong to the tropical or sub-tropical parts of the world, several species being commonly cultivated in Australia. The Australian species, *E. vespertilio*, is no exception, and is mainly found growing in the monsoonal areas of north and north-east Australia. It extends to the rain forest of the east coast and to the dry Centre, and south to near Oodnadatta in South Australia, but is essentially a tree of the dry, sclerophyll forests of the north. In common with several other trees of the monsoonal regions, it drops its leaves at the end of the "Dry" (early summer), flowers, and then produces new leaves.

In the east coast forests the tree is sometimes tall and upright to nearly 33 m in **height,** but elsewhere, and in cultivation, it is only small, seldom exceeding 10 m. It is variable in habit, foliage, and colour of flowers, but is often sparsely branched with little spread. **Bark** is slightly rough, and attractively marked with longitudinal lines or slits on its surface. The **branches** are covered with sharp, woody prickles that resemble rose thorns. The unusual **leaves** are pinnate, consisting of 3 leaflets, and are borne on long petioles. They occur in two distinct shapes, one resembling the extended wings of a bat, from which the common name is derived.

Flowers are large, curved, and pea-shaped, the colour varying from pink to a brilliant orange-red. These are prominently displayed in axillary racemes on stems devoid of leaves, and are very conspicuous, particularly in the open forests of their native habitat where they can be seen standing above the dry undergrowth. The oval-shaped, bean-like **seeds** are a glossy red or yellow, and are contained in pods 5–8 cm long. The Aborigines used the seeds for making necklaces.

The **timber** is soft and spongy, and was used by the Aborigines for making shields.

This tree is occasionally cultivated, and grows quite well as far south as Adelaide, but has rarely been known to produce flowers in that city. A better known species in cultivation is *E. variegata* syn. *phlebocarpa* from northern Queensland. This has been grown for many years and has been cultivated as "Indian Coral Tree" (*E. indica*).

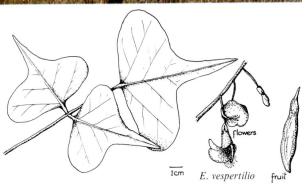

1cm *E. vespertilio* flowers fruit

POWDER-BARKED WANDOO

Eucalyptus accedens W. V. Fitzg. MYRTACEAE

"Powder-Barked Wandoo" is a member of the well-known *Eucalyptus* genus, and is found only in Western Australia. It is a tree usually found on laterite gravelly soils particularly at elevations and is not uncommon in the Darling Range, extending to the relatively dry sclerophyll woodlands of the inland slopes and nearby plains.

Eucalypts are the dominant tree species of the Australian continent, being found in every environment except the very arid deserts of the Inland, and the pure tropical rain forests of parts of the east coast. Within these vastly differing environments many forms occur, from tall forest giants such as "Mountain Ash" to small, stunted, or shrubby "Mallees." Various names have been given to the different types such as "Bloodwoods," "Stringybarks," "Boxes," "Peppermints," "Marlocks," and so on. There are more than five hundred recorded species, although these hybridize quite freely within certain botanical groups, sometimes making positive identification difficult.

Eucalypts are valued throughout the world for ornament, hardwood timber, and conservation purposes, particularly in arid lands.

The genus is characterized by the **flowers** which are without petals and are covered before opening by an operculum or cap. It is this feature which gives the genus its name, "eu"—meaning "well," and "kalyptos"—meaning "covered." This operculum appears in many different shapes in the various species.

The operculums of the "Powder-Barked Wandoo" are a simple, smooth, domed shape. The tree itself is medium-sized, **15–25 m high,** often with a well-branched crown and slightly leaning **trunk,** and a pale orange-coloured **bark** covered with a smooth talc-like powder. It flowers in early summer.

WANDOO *E. wandoo* Blakely syn. *E. redunca* Schau. var. *elata.* Benth., a tree of similar areas of Western Australia, but usually on heavier clay soils, resembles *E. accedens* in appearance except that the **bark** is not powdery and is coloured white or mottled grey. Its botanical features are not similar. The hard **timber** is noted for its durability.

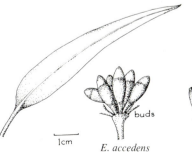

1cm

E. accedens

MARRI

Eucalyptus calophylla R.Br. MYRTACEAE

The "Marri" is one of the largest and commonest trees of the "Jarrah" and "Karri" forests of south-west Western Australia. In the northern and eastern limits of its range, however, it is considerably reduced in stature.

Sometimes known as "Port Gregory Gum" it extends along the coastal regions from Port Gregory near the Murchison River in the north to Cape Riche in the south, and inland to slightly beyond the "Jarrah" country. Within this habitat it favours light sandy soils, particularly near the coast.

"Marri" is a true Bloodwood, possessing friable **bark,** characteristic **leaf** with parallel lateral nerves which spread from the midrib almost at right angles, and umbels of **flowers** arranged in large panicles. The operculum (bud cap) has a tendency to hang on after the flower opens. Urn-shaped **fruits** are large and woody. **Timber** is pale and straight grained.

The tree is a handsome ornamental specimen, reaching **over 35 m high** under favourable conditions, with a dense, spreading crown which gives ample shade. The large pink or, more often, white **flowers** are prominently displayed above the foliage, and occur in masses which make a fine sight in summer.

It is an excellent tree for apiarists.

WESTERN AUSTRALIAN RED FLOWERING GUM, *E. ficifolia* F. Muell. This tree closely resembles the "Marri" but is usually much smaller. It is well known throughout the world as an ornamental flowering specimen tree, although many of the garden-grown flowering gums of today are hybrids between *E. ficifolia* and *E. calophylla*. **Flowers** of the true *E. ficifolia* are usually a vivid vermilion, although flower colours now vary considerably in the pink to red range. These occur from November to February.

Its natural occurrence, near Albany in Western Australia, is very restricted, and the tree is seldom seen under natural conditions.

Both trees are best suited to non-limy soils in a temperate climate.

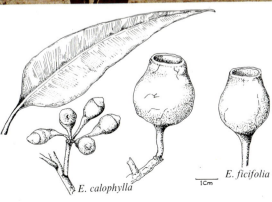

E. calophylla   *E. ficifolia*

1Cm

RIVER RED GUM

Eucalyptus camaldulensis Dehnh.   MYRTACEAE

"River Red Gum" is the most widespread, the best known, and probably the best loved of all the Australian eucalyptus trees.

Artists and photographers have further enhanced its popularity by featuring it so often in their work that it has become almost a symbol of the Australian landscape.

The tree occurs in all States of Australia except Tasmania, usually following the banks of streams. Indeed, in dry open country a watercourse can easily be traced by simply following the line of the "River Red Gum."

It is a variable tree and appears in quite a number of different forms. Typically it is a **large**, gnarled, and wide-spreading tree of great character. The main **trunk** is thick, 1–2 m in diameter, with rough **bark** at the base but smooth and mottled above, usually grey and brown or cream in colour, often beautifully marked. Foliage varies from green to blue-green, the **leaves** often long and narrow, some forms distinctly weeping. Buds and **fruits** also vary throughout its range. **Flowers** are small, creamy-white, and usually occur in summer months.

In northern and central Australia, the tree has a slender, smooth, white **trunk** and a more sparsely foliaged crown. It is this form which is often mistaken for "Ghost Gum" (*E. papuana*).

"River Red Gum," despite its natural habit of following watercourses, is very easy to grow under other conditions. It is an ideal tree for farms, giving shade and shelter to stock, and feed can be grown right up to the trunk, but it has a bad habit of dropping limbs —particularly during hot weather—without warning and should not be planted too close to dwellings.

In northern Western Australia another tree, the **FLOODED GUM,** *E. rudis*, Endl. occurs in association with and could be easily mistaken for "River Red Gum," although in the south, this tree has a rough, fibrous **bark,** and is easily distinguished. This tree should not be confused with the eastern "Flooded Gum" (*E. grandis*), a giant, shaft-like tree of the Queensland and New South Wales forests (see p. 104).

E. camaldulensis

LEMON-SCENTED GUM

Eucalyptus citriodora Hook.   MYRTACEAE

Well known in cultivation owing to its adaptability and its ornamental appearance, "Lemon-Scented Gum" has a naturally confined habitat range (Queensland). Occurring between Mackay and Maryborough along the coast, it extends some 300 km inland, and is also found in a limited area of the Atherton Tableland.

A feature of a number of eucalypts is their bark. Many of the smooth-barked species, particularly just after deciduating usually in late summer, assume mottled colourations which are often very beautiful. Others have smooth, polished, brown bark, like the "Gimlet Gum" (*E. salubris*), or rough, furrowed bark like the "Ironbark" group, but it is always an attractive feature of the tree.

"Lemon-Scented Gum" is no exception, being a particularly graceful tree with a long, shaft-like **trunk,** the **bark** a smooth greyish-white or a lovely pinkish colour in some specimens. It is one of the "Bloodwoods," and a valuable **timber** tree, **reaching 45 m high** under favourable conditions. The crown is usually symmetrical with sparse, but graceful and rather drooping, foliage.

Juvenile **leaves** are rough and hairy, but become long and smooth, narrow to broadly lanceolate, at maturity. The oil in the leaves is rich in citronella which has a commercial use as well as giving the foliage a pleasant lemon aroma, especially when crushed.

Flowers are white and, although not spectacular, appear in quite large, attractive clusters in October-November.

SPOTTED GUM *E. maculata* Hook. is a near relation which is often visually difficult to distinguish from "Lemon-Scented Gum." Usually it is more densely branched and has a mottled or spotted grey **bark,** but the true test is the oil in the **leaves,** which have no lemon scent when crushed. This species is widespread from Queensland to eastern Victoria, where the "Spotted Gum" forests are a feature of parts of the landscape.

Both species are easily grown provided frosts are not severe and rainfall exceeds about 400 mm. They are both rapid growers.

E. citriodora   *E. maculata*

SUGAR GUM

Eucalyptus cladocalyx F. Muell. MYRTACEAE

"Sugar Gum" is probably planted more often on farms as a shelter belt tree than any other eucalypt, at least in the wheat districts of Victoria, South Australia, and Western Australia.

Its natural habitat is quite restricted, the tree being native only to South Australia in the southern Flinders Ranges, on Kangaroo Island, and, as a dwarfed form, on Eyre Peninsula. Climate is temperate with hot dry summers and cool to mild winters. Rainfall is 350–600 mm, most of it falling in winter.

At its best, "Sugar Gum" grows to a **height of 35 m** with a **trunk** 1–2 m in diameter. Its habit is to produce several long, steeply-angled **main branches** from about half-way up the trunk, each branch being clothed in a small umbrageous canopy of shiny foliage. The **bark** is shed in irregular patches, leaving a smooth, mottled effect in colours of orange, brown, grey, and white. The **leaves** are narrow to broad, lanceolate and glossy. The **flowers** which occur in axillary and terminal umbels are creamy yellow in colour, and quite prominently displayed in summer.

"Sugar Gum" recovers from hard cutting very well, and this fact has led to its being periodically pollarded or lopped to produce bushy new growth for windbreak purposes. Unfortunately pollarding these trees has become such a habit that they are treated in this way in many situations where it is quite unnecessary, and the beauty of a well-developed unpruned tree is seldom seen.

Although the "Sugar Gum" is easily grown in the climate and soils suited to wheat growing, many other species form naturally better windbreaks and shelter trees in these areas. **BUSHY SUGAR GUM** *E. cladocalyx* '*Nana*,' a dwarf form of the same species which naturally grows **to 10 m** with a bushy, spreading crown, is one such tree. It is found only in the Marble Range on Eyre Peninsula, South Australia.

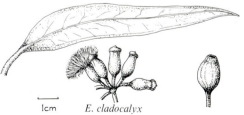

E. cladocalyx

1cm

KARRI

Eucalyptus diversicolor F. Muell.　　　　　　　　　　MYRTACEAE

"Karri" is a tall and majestic forest tree of up to **85 m in height.** It is the tallest tree found in Western Australia where it can be seen dominating the vegetation wherever it grows. The habitat range of "Karri" is restricted to a relatively small area of the south-west, from near Albany to Cape Leeuwin on deep loamy soils where rainfall is in excess of 1000 mm annually. Here, the "Karri" forests are a well-known tourist attraction.

The tree is a true "Gum" with smooth **bark** on a long shaft-like trunk. At the time the old bark is shed, the bark can be seen in varying colours of orange, yellow, grey and white. This feature gives to the tree its specific name of "diversicolor." Its **leaves** are broadly lanceolate, dark green above but paler underneath. The umbels of 3–6 white **flowers** produce a very high-grade honey which is generally recognised as the best in Western Australia.

The **timber** of the "Karri" and of "Jarrah," which it closely resembles, are among Australia's most valued hardwoods. They are deep red in colour, hard, durable, easily worked and, in the case of "Jarrah," resistant to termites and fungi. For this reason they are in much demand for commercial use, such as the construction of flooring boards and joists, railway sleepers, fence-posts, wharves, and jetties. The bushman's test to distinguish between the timber of these two trees is to burn a splinter; if it leaves a white ash it is "Karri;" if it is black or grey it is "Jarrah."

JARRAH, *E. marginata* Sm. is common in south-west Western Australia where rainfall is in excess of 750 mm. Usually a large forest tree, it is found in the sandy soils of the coast-line, extending from Gin Gin, north of Perth (Perth itself was originally a "Jarrah" forest) to as far south as Albany. It is also very prevalent in the laterite or ironstone soils of the Darling Range and elsewhere.

The tree is a "Stringybark." It attains a **height of 40 m** or more at its best, but also occurs in a stunted form only about 2 m high on the stony slopes of the Stirling Range and on rocky outcrops near Albany. **Bark** is dull grey, strong and fibrous and longitudinally fissured. **Leaves** are narrow, 5–8 cm long, a dull, dark green, paler underneath. The **flowers** which occur in umbels of 4–8 during spring and summer are white, but quite attractive although not conspicuous on large trees.

E. diversicolor

E. marginata

1cm.

SAND MALLEE

Eucalyptus eremophila Maid.　　　　　　　MYRTACEAE

A species native only to Western Australia, "Sand Mallee" enjoys an extensive range in the 200–450 mm rainfall zone. It is found in an area bounded approximately by Lake Moore in the north to Gnowangerup in the south, with an eastern limit as far as Balladonia.

Throughout this range the species varies quite appreciably, especially in the flowers and fruits. It is closely related to "Flat-Topped Yate" (*E. occidentalis*), and, in fact, was once described as a variety under that name.

A good deal of its habitat has now been cleared but it can still be found in places forming open thickets, or on the sides of roads, usually in sand, or red alkaline loam.

"Sand Mallee" can be a **single or multi-stemmed tree, 5–8 m in height,** with smooth, polished brown **bark** which is shed in late summer. **Leaves** are narrow with a flattened stalk, grey-green to blue-green in colour.

Flowering period occurs from June to November. The **flowers** are prolific and beautiful and make this tree one of the most ornamental of the flowering mallees, particularly when a good form is chosen. They vary from pale greenish-yellow to deep glowing yellow, or, rarely, a dull red colour. These large flowers droop downwards in clusters of 3–7 arranged on a long, flattened stalk. The operculum is variable, but typically long and curved and narrower at the base than the hypanthium or flower cup. The buds are a polished reddish-brown before the flowers open.

With the ever-increasing interest in growing native trees in Australia, where a small, but ornamental eucalypt is required, "Sand Mallee" could well receive favourable consideration. It is particularly suited to a climate such as Adelaide's or many of the country towns in Australia with a low to moderate rainfall and often alkaline soils. It is also an excellent windbreak species for planting on farms in dry sandy soil areas.

E. macrandra F. Muell., sometimes called the "Long-flowered Marlock," is a very similar free-flowering mallee with bright yellow flowers. It inhabits moist situations from the Stirling Ranges to the Phillips River in Western Australia and tolerates garden watering better than the "Sand Mallee." An ornamental small tree.

E. eremophila

E. macrandra

ILLYARRIE, RED CAP GUM

Eucalyptus erythrocorys F. Muell.   MYRTACEAE

Only a small tree, **3–10 m high,** "Illyarrie" possesses flowers which, even among the eucalypts, are unique and very beautiful. It is this feature which has earned it popularity as a cultivated specimen tree.

Naturally inhabiting quite a restricted area in the Murchison River–Shark Bay coastal districts of Western Australia, it is almost always found on limestone soils with a rainfall of about 350 mm or less.

The juvenile **leaves** of seedlings or new shoots are rough and furry. Seedlings at this stage of leaf growth are slow and difficult to establish, particularly in areas of extreme cold. Young trees should be grown in containers for two years, then planted out. At this stage they mature rapidly to a small, bushy tree with long, rather thick and narrow, usually opposite, curved **leaves** that are a rich glossy green. As the tree develops it grows more slender with sparse, drooping **branches,** and flowers only at the top of the tree. In time, if flowers are a major consideration, it sometimes pays to pollard the tree at ground level, treatment from which it recovers rapidly.

Bark is smooth and white just after deciduating, but turns pale grey as it ages, with occasional persistent patches of a roughish texture.

The **flowers,** either single or in umbels of 2 or 3, consist of a bright red biretta-like cap which falls to reveal stamens at first greenish-yellow, later turning to bright sulphur yellow. These are grouped together in 4 tufts, each individual flower 5 cm or more across. Flowering is often prolific and spectacular, particularly on young trees, with the red operculums and yellow flowers appearing at the one time from March to June. **Fruits** are large and woody, bell-shaped with rather prominent ribbing, the summit a smooth reddish disc for a year or so. The **timber** is quite soft and brittle for a eucalypt, and is easily cut.

"Illyarrie" succeeds on practically any soil in a warm, dry climate. It is now well established as a cultivated specimen, particularly in South and Western Australia where the climate is suitable.

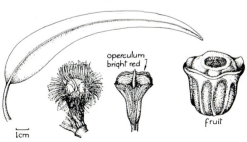

operculum bright red

fruit

1cm

LINDSAY GUM, WHITE MALLEE
Eucalyptus erythronema Turcz.   MYRTACEAE

"Lindsay Gum" has a fairly extensive but scattered range throughout areas of farmland in the drier parts of Western Australia receiving a 300–500 mm rainfall. It is never found in large stands, but is prone to occur in small isolated groups, usually among other species, such as "Gimlet Gum." It favours heavy clay soils which usually indicate land excellent for agriculture.

Although sometimes cultivated, "Lindsay Gum" seldom, if ever, attains the beauty of form which characterises the tree under natural conditions. It is usually found in mallee form, **5–8 m high,** with a broad rootstock supporting **several slender main stems.** These often assume irregular and somewhat contorted outlines which display the tree to its best advantage. The **bark** is a gleaming white (sometimes pinkish) being covered with a smooth, white, talc-like powder, which persists to the smaller branches. When the outer bark decorticates it reveals a pale green smooth surface beneath, which combines with patches of old bark to create a striking effect.

Branches are erect, fairly sparsely foliaged with deep, lustrous green, rather narrow, but thick, **leaves.** These are rich in oil and could have some commercial value. The **flowers** are borne in showy pendulous clusters on long stalks (pedicels). Usually a brilliant red, they are sometimes a creamy-yellow colour, rich in **nectar,** and very attractive to bees. Flowering occurs from October to January. **Fruits** are bell-shaped and about 12 mm in length.

A smaller growing form of this tree occurs north of Perth scattered throughout various districts usually on stony soils. It has been recorded as *E. erythronema* var. *marginata* Benth.

The "Lindsay Gum" is a particularly ornamental flowering eucalypt, well worthy of garden culture in most soils in areas of low to moderate rainfall.

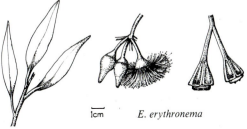

E. erythronema

TASMANIAN BLUE GUM
Eucalyptus globulus Labill.   MYRTACEAE

Sometimes known as "Southern Blue Gum," the common name of "Tasmanian Blue Gum" would seem more apt when one considers that the flowers of this tree have been adopted as Tasmania's floral emblem.

It is a large forest tree, **50–70 m high** under favourable conditions, inhabiting the south-east coast of Tasmania and restricted areas of Victoria at Wilson's Promontory and the Otway Ranges. Climate is cool to mild, with wet winters, annual rainfall up to 1400 mm. "Tasmanian Blue Gum" usually inhabits hilly country or moist valleys in deep, rich soils.

The tree is tall and **straight trunked,** 1–2 m in diameter, with smooth bark except at the base. The **bark** is coloured in patches of grey or grey-blue and sheds in long strips. Juvenile **leaves** and stems are mealy blue and persist for some time. These are broad, opposite and stem clasping, the stems square. Mature leaves, however, are alternate, long and narrow, curved, and a dark glossy green.

The **flowers** which occur from June to November, are quite large and a deep attractive cream. **Timber** is light yellowish-brown, strong, and durable.

This tree is commonly cultivated as "Blue Gum," but is not really suitable for suburban gardens because of the size to which it eventually grows. It is, however, very adaptable as far as soil requirements go, grows extremely rapidly, is quite happy in hot dry climates such as Adelaide's, and can be recommended for parks and large gardens.

"Tasmanian Blue Gum" has been extensively planted overseas as a timber tree, and is well known for its extremely rapid growth, particularly in South Africa.

SOUTHERN BLUE GUM, EURABBIE *E. st johnii* R. T. Bak. syn. *E. bicostata* Maid. Blakely & Simmonds is a closely allied species from the high rainfall eucalypt forests of Victoria and New South Wales, and **MAIDEN'S GUM** *E. maidenii* F. Muell. is another related "Blue Gum" of the high country of those two States.

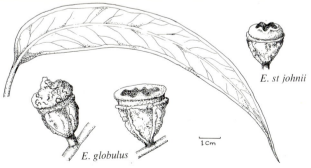

E. globulus

E. st johnii

1 Cm

ROSE GUM, FLOODED GUM
Eucalyptus grandis Hill ex Maid.   MYRTACEAE

One of Australia's finest forest eucalypts is undoubtedly the "Rose Gum," a tall, straight, white-trunked tree of the high rainfall (1000–1800 mm) coastal belt of New South Wales and Queensland. Its main range is from just north of Sydney to south-eastern Queensland, but isolated occurrences are also found near Mackay and on the Atherton tableland in north Queensland.

It is mainly found in the mountain ranges and fertile valleys where soils are deep rich loams often of basalt origin. These soils support sub-tropical rain forest with which "Rose Gum" merges and where it can be seen rising majestically above young rain forest vegetation in the manner portrayed in the picture on the opposite page.

"Rose Gum" grows to a **height** of about **50–60 m** at its best, with a smooth, straight, powdery white **bole** up to 2 m in diameter. At the base it is covered with a short stocking of persistent, rough and fibrous, grey **bark.** The main trunk often extends 30 m or more before the first branches appear. **Leaves** are a glossy green with a paler undersurface, lanceolate, slightly wavy and tapering to a long point. The white **flowers** appear in axillary umbels on flattened stalks, 7–12 flowers per umbel, and the fruits are pear-shaped with protruding valves.

It is a commonly milled tree, being noted for its rose-red **timber** which is softer and lighter than most eucalypt hardwoods. The timber is easily worked and suited to many commercial uses.

"Rose Gum" is a very rapid growing tree which is adaptable to soil and climate where rainfall is adequate. It grows well as far south as Adelaide in the higher rainfall hills and foothills regions where it is sometimes cultivated. Plantations on farmland in northern New South Wales where fertilisers are used have produced 7 m of growth in the first year after planting.

SYDNEY BLUE GUM, *E. saligna* Sm. is another majestic forest tree of similar character. It is found in parts of the southern habitat range of "Rose Gum," with which it is easily confused. Its **fruits** are also very similar to those of "Rose Gum" but are cylindrical or slightly bell-shaped with protruding valves, whilst the **leaves** are narrower. In contrast to "Rose Gum," "Sydney Blue Gum" is seldom found in pure stands and its **timber** is harder and stronger.

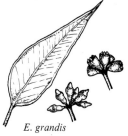
E. grandis

1cm.

E. saligna

BLACK BOX, RIVER BOX

Eucalyptus largiflorens F. Muell.   MYRTACEAE
(syn. *E. bicolor* A. Cunn.)

"Black Box" is a medium to occasionally large-sized tree which is extremely widespread throughout the dry plains of western New South Wales, and extending into Queensland, Victoria, and South Australia. In these parts of New South Wales it is one of the principal eucalypts, often occurring in pure stands, but is also found associated with other species such as "Drooping Myall" (*Acacia pendula*) and the "Native Willow" (*Acacia salicina*).

Although climate is dry, with summer shade temperatures exceeding 38°C, rainfall 250–400 mm and droughts not uncommon, the tree occurs on low-lying depressions and river flats which are subjected to periodic flooding. Soils are usually clay or clay loams with poor drainage.

It is a very common tree in the Upper Murray districts of South Australia, where it sometimes appears in an almost willow-like form, with drooping grey-blue foliage contrasting strikingly with the tree's rough black bark. In such areas as these where stands of "Black Box" still dominate their environment, one is able to realise the great beauty of this often neglected Australian tree.

"Black Box" is a low-branched tree, **10–25 m high,** with a **trunk** up to 1 m in diameter and an open but wide-spreading crown that can provide good shade for stock. The rough **bark** is persistent, often to the smaller **branches,** dark grey to black, and deeply furrowed. **Leaves** are a dull grey-blue in colour, rather narrow and pointed, up to 12 cm long.

Flowers are small and cream or white but prolific, and occur in terminal or axillary panicles of 3–7 in spring and summer.

Timber is pink or reddish brown, heavy and hard, and an excellent fuel.

Despite its dry habitat, "Black Box" only frequents areas where underground water is present and is a particularly good species for planting on soils which become flooded and water-logged after heavy rains. It also tolerates salt and limestone and is a useful species where these hard conditions prevail.

YELLOW GUM, SOUTH AUSTRALIAN BLUE GUM
Eucalyptus leucoxylon F. Muell.　　　　　　　　　MYRTACEAE

"Yellow Gum," or "Blue Gum," as it is known in South Australia, is a fairly common tree of the higher rainfall zones of South Australia, and of north central Victoria.

In South Australia it is well known in the Mount Lofty Ranges, from which it extends as far north as the lower Flinders Range. It also occurs in the South-East as well as to a minor degree on Kangaroo Island and Eyre Peninsula.

In Victoria it is widespread in the north central regions, favouring open woodland in association with mainly eucalypts, such as some of the "Box" group, "Red Ironbark," and several others. A rare drooping, willow-like form occurs near Nhill in Victoria.

Climate is temperate, with cool, often frosty winters, but summer heat exceeding 38°C on occasions. Rainfall is 500–1000 mm.

"Yellow Gum" can be a medium-to-tall and spreading tree, or reasonably slender, **14–28 m in height. Bark** is smooth, white or creamish, mottled grey, rough and persistent at the base. **Leaves** are broad, dull green, and in opposite pairs in the juvenile stage, but up to 15 cm long, alternate, with a prominent central vein at maturity. **Flowers** are quite large, usually in threes, and white. (In the form *E. leucoxylon* '*Rosea*,' they are various shades of attractive pink.) Both forms flower in autumn and winter. **Timber** is pale, tough, strong, and durable.

"Yellow Gum" is a large, ornamental tree preferring heavy-textured, clay soils in its natural habitat, but tolerant of a range of soils including limestone, when cultivated. It is a relatively easy species to grow.

A smaller growing form, *E. leucoxylon* var. *macrocarpa* J. E. Brown, is found in South Australia's South-East. It is a much bushier, lower growing tree, with broad **leaves.** The **flowers** are usually large and often a striking deep pink in colour, occurring from April to June.

PINK GUM *E. fasciculosa* F. Muell. is a tree similar in appearance to "Yellow Gum," and often its close companion, but it favours sandy or stony well-drained soils, and is usually of smaller and more crooked stature.

E. leucoxylon
var. macrocarpa
1cm

YELLOW BOX

Eucalyptus melliodora A. Cunn.　　　　　　　　MYRTACEAE

"Yellow Box" is a common tree of the inland slopes of the Great Dividing Range in Victoria and New South Wales. It is also found to a minor degree on the tablelands of New South Wales and in isolated areas of south-eastern Queensland.

Its typical habitat, however, is found on the gentle slopes of open woodland, occurring in a 350–850 mm rainfall in a temperate climate with cool wet winters and hot, dry summers.

Associated trees in this terrain are other "Box" eucalypts such as "Red Box" (*E. polyanthemos*) and some of the "Ironbark" group, which are closely related. Hybrids between the two groups are not uncommon.

In its low rainfall range "Yellow Box" is usually found in flats and depressions which collect some water during wet periods.

It is quite a large tree, **20–35 m high,** with a rounded, spreading crown, and **trunk** 60–90 cm diameter which extends about one-third of the total height before the first **branches** appear. The brown **bark** is rough, persistent, and friable over the trunk and lower branches but becomes smooth and pale coloured on the smaller branches. The foliage is usually grey-blue, thus contrasting well with the brownish trunk and larger branches to give the tree a handsome overall appearance. However, "Yellow Box" is quite variable in form and is not always seen as described above.

The **flowers** appear in panicles of 3–7 at the ends of the twigs, a feature which is exclusive to only "Box" and "Ironbarks" of the eucalypt genus. They are cream in colour—although there is a rare pink flowering form—and are prolific, making this one of the best **honey** trees of the genus. Flowering occurs from October to February.

Timber is pale yellow, hard, strong, and durable, with a close grain. It is prized as fuel.

"Yellow Box" is a tree which is adaptable to cultivation, preferring good loamy soils, and should be more extensively cultivated as a large tree in parks and gardens in temperate climates with a rainfall exceeding 350 mm.

TALLOW WOOD

Eucalyptus microcorys F. Muell.　　　　　　　MYRTACEAE

"Tallow Wood" is a large forest tree, common in northern coastal New South Wales and southern Queensland. It is usually found in hilly or mountainous country where humidity is high, and rainfall 900–1500 mm annually (most of it falling in summer).

This eucalypt is unusual in that it is sometimes found as an overstorey species in true rain forest. Favouring a warm temperate to sub-tropical climate, it also occurs in the tablelands of New South Wales in areas of frosts and snow. Frequent companions of "Tallow Wood" are "Sydney Blue Gum" (*E. saligna*) and "Blackbutt" (*E. pilularis*).

A mature tree reaches **30–50 m;** it has a long straight **trunk** and compact crown; the first **branches** appear at a point about two-thirds the total height. A lovely feature of the tree is the brown persistent **bark,** which is soft and spongy, fibrous, and deeply furrowed, with corky patches. **Leaves** are bright, shiny green, rather broadly lanceolate, and sharply pointed. The **flowers,** small and white, appear in axillary or terminal panicles from July to November. The bark colour and leaves make it an easily distinguished tree amongst its forest companions.

"Tallow Wood" **timber** is well known and prized as a handsome flooring. It is yellowish, or light brown, strong, hard, and durable. The greasy surface makes it easy to work and polish and it has many commercial uses.

This tree grows quite well on good soils in the cool Mount Lofty Ranges near Adelaide, which is well outside its natural occurrence. It forms a handsome specimen tree, at least while relatively young, often growing more spreading, sometimes multistemmed, with a dense, rich green canopy of foliage.

BASTARD TALLOW WOOD *E. planchoniana* F. Muell. is a similar tree from much the same areas, but with thick, rather broad **leaves,** and much larger, entirely different **flowers** and **fruits.**

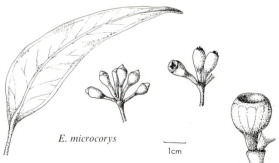

E. microcorys
1cm
E. planchoniana

COOLABAH, COOLIBAH

Eucalyptus microtheca F. Muell. MYRTACEAE

"Coolabah" is an inland tree of legendary fame.

It is found in the very low rainfall inland areas, occurring in all States except Victoria and Tasmania, but always inhabiting watercourses and depressions, usually with a clay subsoil. "Coolabah" is also found in the tropical north of Australia where climate is monsoonal.

In central Australia the typical "Coolabah" is a spreading tree with a thick, tough-barked **trunk** to 120 cm in diameter, smooth bark occurring only on the smaller **branchlets.** Its spread is often as great as its **height — 14–20 m.** It is a tree that provides ample shade where it is really needed.

In Western Australia it is common in the Kimberley division and here it occurs in much the same form as that just described. It extends south as far as the Murchison River area, and it is in this southern extremity of its range that it appears with a smooth, powdery white **bark** covering the trunk and branches, and could justifiably be judged a different species by the observer. This tree was known by the Aborigines as "Yathoo" or "Callaille."

"Coolabah" **timber** is the hardest of all the eucalypt timbers, extremely strong, and termite-resistant. It is typically a dark brown colour but is traversed by whitish threads in the dense, interlocked grain.

The **leaves** are dull and leathery, lanceolate to oblong. In common with most tropical trees the small cup-shaped **fruits** are shed each year after flowering, making **seed** difficult to collect. The creamy-yellow **flowers** are produced in summer.

GREY BOX *E. tectifica* F. Muell. is another Western Australian tree of the Kimberleys. It is very similar in its general appearance to the rough-barked "Coolabah." This tree, however, is seldom seen near watercourses and depressions, as it inhabits the stony rises and hills of the same regions. Its fragile **fruits** are much larger, but decid150te each year also, and are therefore not always available for identification.

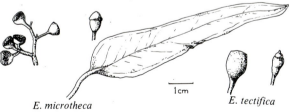

E. microtheca   1cm   *E. tectifica*

WOOLLYBUTT, MELALEUCA GUM

Eucalyptus miniata A. Cunn. MYRTACEAE

One of the larger eucalypts of northern tropical Australia, "Woollybutt" is found in a monsoonal climate with a 750–1500 mm rainfall, practically all of which occurs from December to April.

It extends from the northern Kimberleys in Western Australia, through the Northern Territory and into northern Queensland, usually favouring sandstone or quartzite soils, often in association with "Darwin Stringybark" (*E. tetrodonta* F. Muell.).

The name "Woollybutt" has originated from the persistent **bark** on the lower portions of the tree. This bark on it and on another northern species, *E. phoenicea* F. Muell, is quite different from that of any other of the *Eucalyptus* genus. It consists of numerous thin papery flakes, which, after decay has taken place, remain on the lower parts of the trunk, like pale brown netting.

The tree itself attains a **height of 14–30 m** but often less, with wide-spreading branches, the first branches occurring at about 7 m. The upper portion of the **trunk** and the **branches** is smooth and whitish; the small branchlets are powdery white. These contrast vividly with the broad green **leaves** and spectacular flowers.

The **flowers** are a feature of the tree. These are an intense orange-vermilion (hence the name *miniata*, meaning orange-flowered), quite large individually, and occurring in umbels of 3–7. The flower calyx is also a powdery white.

The tree blooms freely when quite young and small, displaying flowers where they can be easily admired. It flowers in June-July.

Timber is red and hard, but not of high quality, although it is used for milling purposes in the Darwin area.

This tree rivals "W.A. Red Flowering Gum" (*E. ficifolia*) for floral beauty, and should certainly be used as an ornamental flowering tree where climate is suitable.

Little is known of its adaptability to cultivation in more temperate climates.

GNAINGAR *E. phoenicea* F. Muell. is a smaller tree up to **10 m high** which is also noted for its lovely red flowers of up to 16 in each umbel. These are on slender pedicels, thus differing from those of the "Woollybutt" which are without stalks.

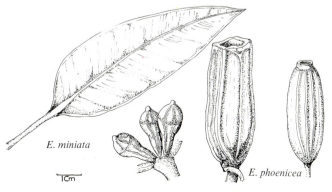

E. miniata

1cm

E. phoenicea

MESSMATE STRINGYBARK, MESSMATE
Eucalyptus obliqua L'Her. MYRTACEAE

"Messmate Stringybark" is a tall forest tree common to mountainous and high rainfall country in the cooler temperate regions of Australia, especially Victoria and Tasmania. It is also found in South Australia, particularly in the Mount Lofty Ranges where it is one of the dominant natural trees, in New South Wales, and to a lesser extent in southern Queensland.

It occurs in the 750–1250 mm rainfall areas where climate is dry and mild in summer, but cold, wet, and often frosty in winter and early spring. The tree is often found in pure stands and where these are allowed to remain on cleared land, they add an attractive feature to the landscape. Parts of the Mount Lofty Ranges near Adelaide depend almost entirely on stands of "Stringybark" for their character and natural beauty.

The tree itself is usually straight and tall, **35–70 m high,** with a **trunk** approximately two-thirds the total height, and 1–3 m (in large trees) in diameter. **Bark** is persistent, rough, and fibrous, brown, but grey coloured when old.

Leaves are long and broadly lanceolate, thick, and dark green on both sides. The new leaves and tips are a lovely bronze colour, often adding an attraction to young trees which is quite delightful, particularly when enhanced by the early morning or late evening sun.

The tree flowers abundantly in summer, the **flowers** being small and cream coloured.

"Messmate Stringybark" timber is one of Australia's most important commercial timbers; it is particularly vital to the economy of Victoria and Tasmania. It is known as Australian or Tasmanian Oak and is used extensively for oak flooring as well as other structural work and furniture, and for pulp manufacture. The **timber** is brown or creamy-brown in colour, hard, straight grained, and easily worked.

GIANT MALLEE, RED MALLEE, OIL MALLEE

Eucalyptus oleosa F. Muell.　　　　　　　　　MYRTACEAE

Eucalyptus oleosa is widespread throughout the drier regions of southern temperate Australia, extending from New South Wales in the east to Western Australia in the west. In common with many trees not restricted to a localised habitat, it occurs in many forms which are quite variable in appearance. Some varieties are known by a separate name, e.g. *E. oleosa* var. *plenissima* C. A. Gardn.

Some forms of *E. oleosa* have hybridized with associated species such as *E. foecunda* Schauer., and sometimes a positive identification is difficult, even for the trained botanist. Closely related trees include the smooth-barked "Merrit" (*E. flocktoniae* Maid.) and "Redwood" (*E. socialis* F. Muell. ex Miq. syn. *E. transcontinentalis* Maid. syn. *E. oleosa* var. *glauca* Maid.) and the rough, scaly-barked "Yorrel" or "Red Morrel" (*E. longicornis* F. Muell.).

E. oleosa appears as a small, many-stemmed mallee, as a large tree of mallee habit and occasionally as a slender single-stemmed tree.

Bark is usually grey and smooth, but rough at the base of the tree, or quite rough on the **trunk** and main **branches. Leaves,** too, are variable, often blue-green (glaucous) but sometimes bright green and shining. **Flowers** which vary from pale cream to a very lovely pale lemon yellow, as in *E. socialis*, are usually abundant and attractive. Flowering time is variable, usually from May to December.

It is the **fruits** which retain individual characteristics throughout the species. These are typically smooth and globular with a narrow rim, and deeply included valves with protruding needle-like points. Operculums are considerably variable as can be seen from the sketches.

The specific name (*oleosa*) originated from the large oil content of the leaves, this tree being particularly useful for the production of eucalyptus oil.

Although seldom cultivated, good forms of this tree can be quite ornamental, and are particularly useful in dry alkaline soils in conditions where many trees are difficult to grow. It is a good honey tree.

 E. oleosa   1cm   *E. socialis*   *E. longicornis*

GHOST GUM

Eucalyptus papuana F. Muell.   MYRTACEAE

The "Ghost Gum," a tree made famous by Aboriginal painters, has an extensive range over northern Australia, particularly the Northern Territory, as well as inhabiting savannah woodland near Port Moresby in Papua.

Although principally a tree of the tropics, where climate is monsoonal, it is in the dry southern parts of its range in the Northern Territory and to a lesser extent, Queensland, where this tree has earned its fame. Here it is often the only notable tree occurring over wide areas. It is in this part of its habitat that it contrasts vividly with the colourful landscape, and has become a feature of the artist's brush.

Under these drier more temperate conditions the "Ghost Gum" is usually found inhabiting river flats subjected to periodic flooding. It is in these situations where the "River Red Gum," *E. camaldulensis*, also flourishes, and is often mistaken for "Ghost Gum" in these areas, where it appears with very similar superficial characteristics.

Mature trees vary considerably within the habitat range, from a slender **7 m up to 25 m,** and are well branched and spreading. In the drier zones the **trunk** is often slender and reaches 5 m or more before the first limbs appear. The **bark** is lustrous, smooth, and white, and contrasts with the **leaves,** which are deep green and shining.

The overall beauty of the tree is enhanced still further by the pendulous habit of the **branchlets.**

The small white **flowers** and urn-shaped **fruits** do not remain for long on the tree and for this reason **seed** of this species is not readily obtained.

Timber is pale red, dense, and hard.

Although it favours a tropical climate, the "Ghost Gum" has such an extensive range embracing a number of different conditions, that it could possibly respond very well to cultivation in other areas.

Photograph by courtesy of R. J. Shinkfield

1 cm

SNOW GUM

Eucalyptus pauciflora Sieb. var. *alpina* Ewart.   MYRTACEAE
(syn. *E. niphophila* Maid et Blakely).

As its common name implies, "Snow Gum" is native only to the high altitudes (1300–2300 m) of Victoria and New South Wales where snow persists throughout the winter and early spring months.

It forms the limit of tree vegetation in these alpine areas and under the hardest climatic conditions of the region takes on its most attractive, if contorted, form. At lower altitudes and under less harsh conditions, however, it grows erect but loses its characteristic aged appearance. Here, other related species, "White Sally" (*E. pauciflora*) and "Black Sally" (*E. stellulata*) are also encountered, but these are never found above the 1800 m mark.

The tree itself is usually mallee-like, **5–8 m high,** with a broad crown of foliage and a crooked, smooth-barked **trunk.** At all times of the year it is astonishingly attractive, especially when the trunk appears in striking colours of brown, gold, sienna, and red.

During December to February the "Snow Gum" flowers profusely, producing its white **flowers** in umbels of 3–7. The thick, usually lanceolate **leaves,** buds and **fruits** are often quite glaucous, giving a waxy appearance which adds to the attraction of the species.

Quite frequently on the high plains, areas of "Snow Gum" are burnt by bush-fires, many of them regenerating quite well from the base. Others, however, succumb, and after years of exposure to gales, blizzards, and associated elements, they become stark, weathered skeletons of their former selves. These grow white with age and stand like enormous trees of driftwood in the landscape, contrasting vividly, particularly in summer, with the dark green and brown surrounds of the vegetation of alpine Australia.

WHITE SALLY *E. pauciflora* Sieb. has a wider distribution and extends from New South Wales and Victoria to the south-east of South Australia, as well as Tasmania, where it is found at elevations, and near sea-level. It can grow into quite a large, spreading tree.

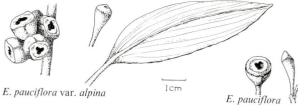

E. pauciflora var. alpina   1cm   E. pauciflora

MOUNTAIN ASH

Eucalyptus regnans F. Muell.　　　　　　　　　MYRTACEAE

"Mountain Ash" is Australia's, and one of the world's tallest trees, specimens having been found of over 115 m in height.

It is a giant, shaft-like tree of the high rainfall country of Victoria and Tasmania. In Victoria it is found in the mountains of the east with a restricted occurrence in the Otway Range, and in Tasmania, in the north-east, south-east, and the Huon and Derwent valleys.

Climate is cool to mild in summer with cold wet winters, and some snow in the higher altitude range. Annual rainfall is 750–1500 mm, most of which falls in winter.

The best trees are found in the mountain valleys in deep, rich, moist soils, usually in pure stands. A pure stand of these giants with an understorey of tree ferns and ground cover shrubs is a sight to be long remembered by all lovers of the Australian bushland. On the poorer soils it occurs with other eucalypt species such as "Messmate" (*E. obliqua*).

Usual tree heights range from **50–80 m.** The **trunk** is long and straight, up to 3 m in diameter at the base, with a sparse, open crown. The **bark** is rough and persistent at the base and up to 16 m, but smooth thereafter, white or pale grey in colour, and is shed in long ribbons, often up to 10 m in length, which hang from the trees. Adult **leaves** are long, narrow, and curved, and a smooth, shining green on both sides. The small white **flowers** bloom mainly in late summer.

"Mountain Ash" is one of Australia's most valuable timber trees. The **timber** is used extensively in joinery, furniture, and various structures, as well as in the pulping industry. Like "Messmate" it is known as Australian Oak or Tasmanian Oak. It has a pale brown or cream-coloured open texture with a straight grain, which is easily worked and dressed, and is hard and durable.

There has been little attempt to grow this species in Australia, except in State forests.

CANDLEBARK

Eucalyptus rubida Deane and Maid.   MYRTACEAE

At its best "Candlebark" is one of Australia's loveliest gum trees. Although more prevalent in the eastern States, some of the best specimens are seen in parts of the Mount Lofty Ranges near Adelaide. In the richer soils and in gullies near creeks, majestic specimens with gleaming white bark remain in solitary splendour, **35 m or more high,** and perfect in every detail.

The tree is native to the cooler, hilly areas of New South Wales, Victoria, Tasmania, and South Australia where rainfall usually exceeds 750 mm and soils are alluvial or granite.

It can be a tall straight tree with an open crown and powdery white bark on the trunk and branches, or, often in poorer soils, a relatively small thick tree with a somewhat crooked, or leaning, trunk, and sometimes a multi-coloured bark rather akin to that of the "River Red Gum."

The **trunk** is 1 m or more in diameter with a smooth **bark** which peels off in flakes leaving the bole a pure white which darkens to a salmon pink before deciduating again.

Leaves are rather broad and pointed, glaucous in the juvenile stages, and often remaining so, or sometimes becoming a dull green when mature. **Flowers** are in axillary umbels of three, and are small and white. **Timber** is pink or red and worthless except for fuel.

This tree is best suited to cool, wet, elevated conditions in a temperate climate, where it makes a large specimen tree of striking beauty, particularly after the old bark has just been shed. It flowers in summer and is a good honey tree.

MANNA GUM *E. viminalis* Labill. is a closely related companion of the "Candlebark." This is a tall forest tree that prefers cool mountain valleys and is found in all southern and eastern States. It is usually **35–50 m high;** the long shaft-like **trunk,** 1–2 m in diameter, has rough, ribbony **bark** at the base, but is smooth and white above. Ribbony scaling bark often hangs in long strands from the upper branches. The tree has a fairly open crown, with rather drooping **branchlets,** and long narrow **leaves.**

This is an ornamental species suited to cool, mountainous situations.

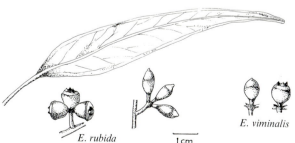

E. rubida *E. viminalis*

1 cm

SALMON GUM

Eucalyptus salmonophloia F. Muell. MYRTACEAE

Widespread throughout the eastern goldfields and agricultural areas of Western Australia, "Salmon Gum" extends from some distance east of the Norseman–Kalgoorlie area to a western limit about 160 km or so from Perth. Its northern limit is near Mullewa, and its southern limit, the Oldfield River to Salmon Gums.

The tree is found in open woodland usually on red, loamy, alkaline soils supporting an understorey of "Blue-Bush," *Acacia, Eremophila,* and other low-growing vegetation. Associated trees are mainly *Eucalyptus* species, such as "Gimlet" (*E. salubris*), "Morrel" (*E. gracilis*), and several others. Its presence has always been considered an indication of good soil well suited to agriculture, although it still remains a feature of the landscape in the 200–250 mm rainfall areas that are too dry for growing crops.

"Salmon Gum" is an exceptionally handsome, erect, and shapely tree growing up **to 28 m high,** with a long, smooth-barked **trunk,** and small umbrageous crown. Where single specimens have been allowed to remain in cleared areas, the tree is more wide-spreading, and gives ample shade.

The smooth **bark,** as with so many trees of the genus, is a feature of the tree. Light reddish-brown when first exposed, it changes to a salmon pink in summer and then to pale grey or white before shedding in autumn to winter. **Leaves** 7–12 cm long, are a deep lustrous green, and give the tree a burnished or lacquered effect. The small white **flowers** which occur in summer are rich in **nectar,** making the tree an excellent species for apiarists.

The roots of "Salmon Gum" are very shallow and wide-spreading.

This is a fine, ornamental tree which should be more widely cultivated in dry areas.

DUNDAS MAHOGANY *E. brockwayi* C. A. Gardn. is a tree of similar size and general appearance, found only in a restricted area near Norseman. It can be distinguished by its **bark** which is usually paler, although it is deep red when new.

Photograph by courtesy of G. D. Watton

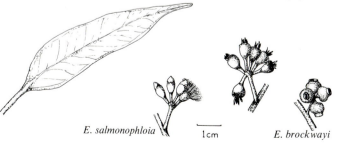

E. salmonophloia   1cm   E. brockwayi

GIMLET GUM

Eucalyptus salubris F. Muell.   MYRTACEAE

The "Gimlet Gum" is one of the best known and commonest trees of the Western Australian eastern agricultural and eastern goldfields districts. It has a distribution northwards as far as Mullewa, and southwards to the Ravensthorpe area.

The tree almost always inhabits rich, red, alkaline, clay loams, often in open woodland association with "Salmon Gum" (*E. salmonophloia*). Rainfall is 200–500 mm. In the low rainfall goldfields areas it is never stunted as might be expected, but is seen as a fine tree which, with "Salmon Gum," and sometimes other eucalypts, dominates the landscape.

"Gimlet Gum" is easily recognised by its smooth, clean, varnished, red-brown to greenish-brown **bark,** and often fluted, or spirally twisted **trunk,** especially in the younger trees. Mature trees reach **28 m in height** with usually an upright, regular habit, and a bushy, well-proportioned crown of glistening, dark green foliage. The upper **branches** are smooth and reddish in colour. **Flowers** are white and produced in axillary umbels, and the **fruits** are quite small. **Flowering** time is variable, from March to October.

SILVER-TOPPED GIMLET *E. campaspe* S. le M. Moore is a closely related species confined to the eastern goldfields area of Western Australia.

It is a smaller tree, up **to 12 m high,** with a wide-spreading crown in solitary specimens, but where it grows in thickets, as it often does, the tree appears in a very slender, sparsely crowned, whipstick formation.

This tree is very easily distinguished from the "Gimlet" by the whitish powder on the upper **branches,** and its blue-green (glaucous) **leaves.** The **fruits,** also, are larger.

The pale brown **timber** of both "Gimlets" is very hard, durable, and straight grained, and has been used extensively for tool handles, etc. The tree flowers in summer.

Both trees are adaptable, and extremely useful for both ornamental and shelter planting, particularly in dry areas. "Silver-Topped Gimlet" is used as a street tree in inland towns.

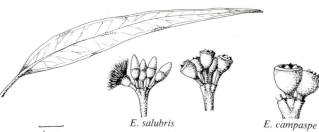

E. salubris   *E. campaspe*

1cm

SALT RIVER YATE, SALT RIVER MALLET
Eucalyptus sargentii Maid.   MYRTACEAE

A group of tough Western Australian eucalypts have been given the common name of "Yate," or "Mallet." "Yate" is an Aboriginal word for some hard-grained timber trees of the Eyre coastal plain. This group has certain similar characteristics of flowers and fruits such as long horn-shaped operculums, erect stamens within, and the usually flattened common flower stalk supporting each umbel of flowers. Some trees in this related group do not bear this common name, although the botanical features are similar, (e.g. "Sand Mallee"—*E. eremophila*—see p. 96).

"Salt River Yate" is a tree of fairly restricted occurrence found near salty waterways of the central wheatlands; **10–15 m in height,** usually with a single upright **trunk** and rather spreading crown. **Bark** is dark, rough and flaky at the base of the tree; thereafter smooth and greenish-brown, and reddish on smaller **branches.** The narrow **leaves,** 7–15 cm long, are a lustrous green. It flowers prolifically in spring, with creamy-white **flowers** in umbels of 3–7 on a common slender peduncle or stalk. A hardy, ornamental tree, useful for salty soils where few others will survive.

BROWN MALLET *E. astringens* Maid. is closely related, growing in the southern agricultural districts eastwards to Esperance and beyond where it also occurs in mallee form. **FLAT-TOPPED YATE, SWAMP YATE** *E. occidentalis* Endl. is usually a 14–28 m tree found in alluvial flats and depressions of the southern wheatlands. It is easily distinguished by a flat-topped, spreading crown, and is also a good tree for salty soils. Other trees in this group include: **SWAMP MALLET** *E. spathulata* Hook. Small, ornamental tree, with very narrow, attractive leaves. Found in swampy flats in parts of the wheatbelt. **BLUE MALLET** *E. gardneri* Maid. Ornamental, blue-foliaged, to 10 m. in height. Often found in whipstick thickets on gravelly soils of eastern wheatlands. **YATE GUM** *E. cornuta* Labill., the true "Yate." A large rough-barked timber tree of the higher rainfall south-western areas. Grows well near the sea coast. **BUSHY YATE** *E. lehmanii* Preiss. Dense, bushy, to 10 m high; extends from Albany to beyond Cape Arid. Massed heads of greenish flowers in winter and spring. **WARTY YATE** *E. megacornuta* C. A. Gardn., a rare 10 m tree of the Ravensthorpe Range.

E. sargentii   1cm   *E. astringens*   *E. occidentalis*

RED IRONBARK, MUGGA

Eucalyptus sideroxylon A. Cunn. ex Woolls.   MYRTACEAE

"Red Ironbark" is a medium-sized tree found commonly in undulating woodland extending from north central Victoria through the western slopes of the Great Dividing Range in New South Wales to southern Queensland. It is usually found in poor shallow soils with a 350–650 mm rainfall and temperate climate, except in the northern extremities of its range where it is subtropical. Associated trees include "Yellow Box" (*E. melliodora*), "Yellow Gum" (*E. leucoxylon*), "Red Stringybark" (*E. macrorhyncha*), and several other trees of the "Box" and "Ironbark" group.

There are also scattered occurrences in the higher rainfall coastal areas of northern Victoria and southern New South Wales.

The "Ironbark" trees are a very distinctive group of Australian eucalypts, easily recognized by the hard, deeply furrowed, rough **bark,** which is dark grey or almost black in colour, and persists to the smaller branches. Foliage is usually a dull grey or grey-blue and provides a handsome contrast to the dark **trunk.** The **timber** is valued for its strength and durability, being hard and dense with an interlocked grain. In "Red Ironbark" the timber is a dark red colour.

"Red Ironbark" is a tree that can reach **33 m in height,** but is usually much less, with a slender **trunk** of no significant height before the first **branches** appear.

A pink flowered form, *E. sideroxylon* '*Rosea*,' is often planted for ornamental purposes. Particularly in its young stages, the combination of grey-blue foliage, black **trunk,** and showy small pink **flowers,** is extremely attractive.

It is an adaptable tree tolerating most soils, including limestone. Flowering time is usually late winter.

NARROW-LEAVED RED IRONBARK *E. crebra* F. Muell. and **BROAD-LEAVED RED IRONBARK** *E. fibrosa* Benth. are somewhat similar trees of coastal Queensland and New South Wales. "Narrow-Leaved Red Ironbark" has a particularly wide distribution extending from along the coast south of Sydney north to Cairns in Queensland, and some 500 km inland to the dry western plains.

E. sideroxylon

1cm.

E. crebra

E. fibrosa

CORAL GUM, COOLGARDIE GUM

Eucalyptus torquata Luehm.　　　　　　　　　MYRTACEAE

"Coral Gum" has a restricted habitat in the Coolgardie–Norseman area of the eastern goldfields of Western Australia, and is far from common even there.

Because of its attractive flowers and shapely habit, however, it has rapidly become a popular and well-known species throughout the drier regions of Australia where it is frequently cultivated, both as a garden and as a street tree.

This tree hybridizes very freely and many garden "cultivars" with an affinity to "Coral Gum" are now being grown. In Kalgoorlie there are many examples of related trees in the streets, each with interesting and beautiful flower variations. One "cultivar" known as *E. 'Torwood'* is seen as a variable tree, but almost always with large clusters of beautiful orange or orange-yellow flowers.

Under natural conditions the "Coral Gum" is a shapely tree, **8–12 m high,** with a dense, spreading crown of blue-green foliage. Its shapeliness under these conditions probably explains why it is so reliable when cultivated.

Bark is dark grey, almost black, rough, and persistent. The very decorative **flowers** hang in abundant, pendulous clusters. They are usually a coral pink colour, but variations occur from creamy yellow to a rich blood red. Flower buds are also very beautiful, being orange-yellow with a ribbed base and enclosed by an attractively shaped, ribbed operculum. These contrast very well with the bluish **leaves.** The tree blooms when very young, produces an abundance of **nectar,** and is an excellent tree for apiarists. It flowers from November to March.

"Coral Gum" is extremely reliable in cultivation provided rainfall is under about 600 mm and frosts are few, but is perhaps seen at its best where rainfall is as low as 200–250 mm. **Flowers** are usually more vivid under very dry conditions. It is not particular as regards soils.

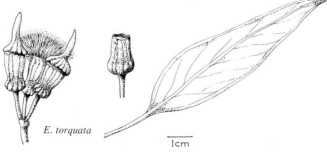

E. torquata

1cm

NATIVE CHERRY

Exocarpos cupressiformis Labill. SANTALACEAE

Throughout the wetter parts of temperate Australia, particularly in hilly country, the conifer-like "Native Cherry" commands attention wherever it is encountered. This tree with its cypress-like foliage, often faintly golden in appearance, contrasts conspicuously with the more sombre greens of the dominant eucalypt and other associated plants of this terrain.

It belongs to the "Sandalwood" family, and in common with most of these plants, is apparently a root parasite, but does not appear to harm the plants from which it feeds. Regenerating freely from root suckers, it is often seen in closely grouped clumps, particularly on road banks where land clearing has missed the native vegetation.

The tree is dense, with a coniferous habit, usually **4–8 m high.** The slender **branches** are covered with rough, scabrous, grey **bark,** and the foliage which consists of **leaves** reduced to scales, resembles the garden cypress in appearance, and is pale green to a golden green in colour.

The minute and inconspicuous **flowers** are produced on stiff, green stalks (peduncles) which swell to a brightly coloured, rounded, cone- or pear-shaped receptacle, which is succulent and edible. These are surmounted by a smaller hard, green **fruit** appearing outside the fleshy receptacle. At about Christmastime they are very decorative when they ripen, and colours on any one tree at the same time vary from green, through yellow and orange, to a bright red.

This lovely little tree should be preserved wherever possible on properties, and is well worth attempts to cultivate it as a specimen tree.

There are about twenty species of *Exocarpos*, all native to the Southern Hemisphere. Apart from "Native Cherry," those endemic to Australia are mainly only shrubby in stature. *Exocarpos sparteus* R. Br. is usually only a single-stemmed shrub, but sometimes a small tree **to 5 m** with long, weeping, broom-like foliage of a pale golden-green colour. It is often seen growing at the base of larger trees where it forms a distinctive and lovely bush plant.

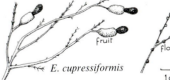
E. cupressiformis — fruit

flowers
1cm

E. sparteus

MORETON BAY FIG

Ficus macrophylla Desf. MORACEAE

"Moreton Bay Fig" is a massive tree inhabiting the rain forests of coastal northern New South Wales to northern Queensland, and inland to the Bunya Mountains.

Most species of *Ficus* are large to gigantic trees belonging to the tropical rain forests of mainly Queensland. Under these conditions, the seeds of some species are lodged in the branches of associated trees where they germinate and send down aerial roots which eventually strangle the host tree on which they began their life.

The genus is distinguished by the fruit (fig) which consists of a fleshy receptacle containing minute flowers on the inner surface; also the branches and leaf stalks when cut, exude a sticky white juice. Several species are very similar in general appearance, particularly when cultivated as park trees, when they form dense, spreading trees which branch to the ground, and cover an area often greater in diameter than their height.

Under forest conditions "Moreton Bay Fig" attains a **height of 50 m.** It has a thick buttressed **trunk** and massive spreading roots often partly visible above the ground. The **bark** is grey and rough, and the **leaves** large, about 20 cm long by 8 cm broad, dark glossy green, and leathery. The undersurface is brownish coloured and displays the vein structure quite prominently. The young buds are protected by stipules which are folded around them and taper to a long point. **Fruits** are globular, purple dotted white, and about 2·5 cm in diameter, on thick stalks.

Once extensively planted by the early settlers who apparently recognized the need for shade trees of this type, "Moreton Bay Fig" is seldom cultivated today. There are many parts of Australia with hot, dry summers where it is easily grown, and where there could hardly be a better tree for park planting. Today the tree is more often grown in pots and used in its seedling stage as a successful indoor plant.

GREEN-LEAVED MORETON BAY FIG *F. watkinsiana* F. M. Bail. is found in similar localities and is very like "Moreton Bay Fig" in appearance. Its **leaves,** however, are green on both surfaces, and the purple **fruits** have a distinct nipple at the apex.

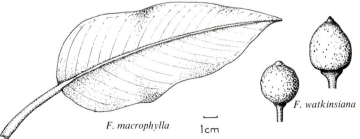

F. macrophylla |—1cm—| *F. watkinsiana*

RUSTY-LEAVED FIG, PORT JACKSON FIG
Ficus rubiginosa Desf. ex Vent.   MORACEAE

"Rusty-leaved Fig" is a very large tree which is restricted to New South Wales and Queensland, being found in the rain forests extending from south of Bateman's Bay to the Darling Downs where it occurs in isolated areas.

Apart from the "Moreton Bay Fig," this tree is perhaps the most commonly seen "Fig" in cultivation, and grows quite easily in relatively harsh, but frost-free conditions. It is easily distinguished from the former by its leaves which are smaller and more round in shape with a velvet rust-coloured undersurface. However, under natural conditions this tree is quite variable in general form and in the amount of rusty tomentum on the foliage.

Usually when cultivated the tree does not attain the massive proportions of the "Moreton Bay Fig," but under natural conditions it is a tree of similar stature. Here it reaches a **height of 50 m** with a large buttressed **trunk** over 2 m in diameter. The **bark** is grey, and the thick branchlets hairy. **Leaves** are elliptical with a blunt point at the apex, dark green and glossy on top, but rusty and hairy underneath. The leaf stalks too, are covered with fine hairs. **Fruits** are oval-shaped, often bluntly pointed, 1–2 cm in diameter, and dotted.

"Rusty-leaved Fig" forms a handsome spreading shade tree of up to 20 m in height, well suited for planting in parks and golf courses throughout most settled parts of Australia.

A variegated form of this tree, *F. rubiginosa* '*Variegata*' is used extensively as a pot and tub plant. When planted for ornament it forms a dense, conical tree of handsome appearance.

SMALL-LEAVED FIG *F. obliqua* Forst. f. syn. *F. eugenioides* F. Muell. is a Queensland species which is scattered throughout many rain forest scrubs of that State. In general appearance it resembles the "Rusty-leaved Fig," although the **leaves** are smaller and more pointed, smooth, and paler green on both surfaces. **Fruits** are small and globular, yellow when ripe.

This tree has been successfully grown as a street tree in Whyalla, South Australia, where soil is dry and very alkaline, and rainfall usually under 300 mm.

F. obliqua

F. rubiginosa

1cm

fruit

CROW'S ASH, AUSTRALIAN TEAK
Flindersia australis R.Br.   RUTACEAE

"Crow's Ash" is a fairly common member of the *Flindersia* genus which, with two exceptions, are large sub-tropical or tropical rain forest trees of Queensland, and in some cases New South Wales, usually growing well over 35 m tall.

The genus commemorates Captain Matthew Flinders and belongs to the same family (*Rutaceae*) as several of Australia's choice dwarf shrubs, such as *Boronia, Correa, Eriostemon*, etc. There are twenty-one recorded species of *Flindersia*, fourteen of these being Australian. In common with several other rain forest genera, odd species are found in dry areas of the continent. In this case, "Leopard Wood" (*F. maculosa*) and *F. strzeleckiana* F. Muell. are dry area species.

The rain forest *Flindersia* are mainly fine timber trees and include the popular and much used "Queensland Maple" (*F. brayleyana* F. Muell.) found in the Atherton districts near Cairns. "Crow's Ash" timber is also used extensively in the building industry.

"Crow's Ash" is a tall, upright, semi-deciduous tree growing **up to 50 m high** with a scaly, brown **bark** on a **trunk** up to 1·5 m in diameter.

The handsome, pinnate **leaves** comprise egg-shaped or elliptical leaflets arranged in opposite pairs, with a single leaflet at the tip. These are dark green, paler underneath, with numerous minute, transparent dots which are prominent when held to the light. **Flowers** are small and white with a brown centre, and occur in dense, terminal panicles in spring months.

The hard, woody **fruits** which remain united at the base, open to expose 4, 5, or 6 valves containing flat, winged **seeds.** The attractively shaped fruit covered with blunt spines when dried forms a fine subject for interior decoration or floral art work.

Many of the rain forest trees, in their search for light, grow tall and shaft-like under natural conditions, but are lower and more spreading when cultivated as single specimens particularly in the cooler southern climates. "Crow's Ash," however, retains its tall, forest habit under these conditions also, and is usually too large for average gardens. It requires rich, moist soils.

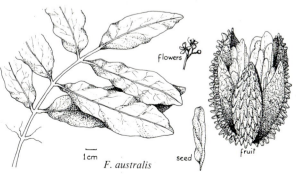

F. australis

LEOPARD WOOD

Flindersia maculosa Benth. RUTACEAE

"Leopard Wood" is a dry area tree belonging to a genus of mainly tropical rain forest species. It is found in the low rainfall areas of northwest New South Wales, extending from near Broken Hill to the western slopes of the Great Dividing Range, and in Queensland, often in association with the "Wilga" (*Geijera parviflora*).

Areas dominated by the "Leopard Wood" are usually only lightly wooded, very often on elevated red sandy soils with an understorey of "Salt Bush" and other associated species. It is also found in heavy soils, although it favours the deep sands in which it grows best.

A curious feature of the tree is its manner of growth in the early stages of its life. Beginning as a tangled mass of long thin branches, it eventually produces a leading shoot which is protected by the tangled branches as it develops to a straight, main stem.

Eventually a graceful medium-sized tree **to 14 m in height** is formed. It has a single **trunk** with handsome spotted or mottled **bark,** the mottled effect being caused by the outer layers falling off in patches. The narrow, opposite **leaves** are 2–7 cm long, occasionally lobed. **Flowers** are white, in terminal panicles, individually small but occurring in showy masses in spring. **Fruit** is a hard capsule, 2·5–4 cm long, and containing flat **seeds,** winged at each end.

The yellow-coloured **timber** has a tough grain but is only useful for indoor use as it deteriorates rapidly when exposed. A pleasant-tasting, amber-coloured gum is exuded in quite large quantities in summer, and this can be made into an excellent adhesive mucilage. The foliage is sometimes used as fodder in times of drought, but the tree is not generally considered a good fodder tree.

"Leopard Wood" is a very ornamental, but seldom cultivated tree, which would probably succeed on many soil types where drainage is good.

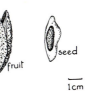

fruit   seed

1cm

WILGA

Geijera parviflora Lindl.　　　　　　　　　　　　　　　　RUTACEAE

"Wilga" is a delightful little tree from the dry areas, found mainly on the western plains of New South Wales and Queensland, but also in northern South Australia and northwest Victoria, often in sandy soils.

The tree is loved by stock which frequently nibble the lower foliage producing a very formal effect among natural trees. A stand of "Wilga" are sometimes the only trees to be seen in an arid landscape. Displayed in this way they are quite striking. Herbivores unfortunately eat many of the young plants before they are able to develop and in some areas the tree has become quite rare.

"Wilga" is usually low growing, **5–8 m high,** and of symmetrical outline, with a dense, rounded crown often wider than its overall height, drooping grey foliage, and a short upright **trunk. Bark** is dark grey to brown.

The long, narrow, linear **leaves** are pleasantly aromatic when crushed. **Flowers** are bell-shaped, small, and white, usually appearing in winter in loose panicles which combine with the grey foliage to create a lovely silvery effect. **Fruiting carpels** are small and globular, containing hard, shiny, black **seeds.**

There are few examples of this tree in cultivation, although in Adelaide, at least, specimens are occasionally encountered. It is fairly slow growing, but deep rooted and permanent, and its ideal shape makes it an excellent tree for planting under overhead service wires, either in the street or elsewhere.

Geijera is an entirely Australian genus, and is limited to five species.

SCRUB WILGA *Geijera salicifolia* Schott. is quite a large, upright, rain forest tree growing **to 28 m,** from the brush forests of New South Wales and Queensland. The **bark** is rough and scaly and the **leaves** lance-shaped, usually broad, but a narrow-leaved form also occurs. The **timber** is useful for various purposes.

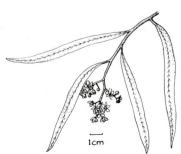

G. parviflora

WHITE BEECH, GREY TEAK

Gmelina leichhardtii F. Muell. VERBENACEAE

A tall, semi-deciduous tree from the coastal scrub forests of the east coast, "White Beech" is found from the Shoalhaven River south of Sydney, to the mountain ranges near Mackay in Queensland. Owing to the demand for its timber it is no longer very prevalent in these areas. Limited to only three Australian species, the genus consists mainly of plants native to tropical Asia, India, and Indonesia.

Under natural rain forest conditions "White Beech" reaches a **height of 40 m** with trunk diameters up to 1·5 m. **Bark** is grey and scaly. The handsome, opposite **leaves,** which are broadly ovate in shape, drop in November, the new leaves appearing soon after. Flowering occurs at this time. On the undersides of the leaves there is a prominent raised network of veins covered with a brown velvety down of fine hairs. This down persists to the young shoots, smaller branchlets, leaf stalks, and flowers.

The fully pedunculate tubular **flowers** are white with blue or violet and yellow markings in the throat, and are borne conspicuously above the foliage in large terminal panicles. **Fruits** are succulent berries, purplish-mauve in colour when ripe, flat-spherical in shape and enclosing a 4-celled, hard stone which contains a small oval **seed** in each cell.

The durable **timber** is valued for many indoor purposes, being easy to work, with an attractive close grain.

"White Beech" is rarely seen in cultivation, but forms an attractive, small specimen tree in drier, cooler climates, and is best suited to a well-drained, moist soil.

The other two species of *Gmelina* in Australia are both native to the tropical north.

NORTH QUEENSLAND WHITE BEECH *G. fasciculiflora* Benth. is found only in Queensland in the Cairns–Atherton districts. It is superficially very similar in general character to "White Beech" but is distinguished by the **flowers** which are in sessile cymes forming the panicles.

The other species, *G. dalrympleana* F. Muell. syn *G. macrophylla* Benth., is also similar but with larger **leaves** up to 25 cm long and fleshy reddish-pink **fruits.** It is found in northern Australia and New Guinea.

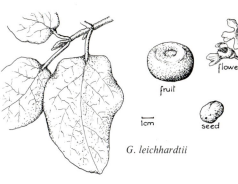

G. leichhardtii

WATER BUSH

Grevillea nematophylla F. Muell.   PROTEACEAE

"Water Bush" is a small inland tree or tall shrub from the dry parts of Western Australia, South Australia, and New South Wales. Although seldom exceeding **5–7 m in height,** it often gives the impression of very great age with its gnarled shape and deeply fissured brown **bark.** It grows under many varying conditions, but is often seen at its best in light, sandy soils.

The genus, *Grevillea*, is an important member of the Australian flora, containing many beautiful flowering plants which range in size from dwarf under-shrubs to (in a few instances) large forest trees. Most species bear quaint and beautiful, brightly coloured **flowers,** often over a long period, and are very decorative in the garden. The genus differs from the closely allied *Hakea* in its flat seeds which are shed each year after flowering, and its shell-like seed follicle. Of the nearly two hundred recorded species, only a very few are found outside Australia.

This particular species grows erect with upright **branches** and usually a narrow head of foliage during its early life. The **leaves** are long and slender, blue-grey in colour, and rather rigid. A tree in full flower in early summer is a magnificent sight with its masses of greenish-cream **flower spikes** in dense racemes, produced mainly towards the ends of the branches. These are full of **nectar** and loved by birds and bees. **Seed follicles** which follow are dark brown when ripe, and about 1 cm across; they contain two flat seeds.

Easily grown from seed, this tree thrives in the drier cities such as Adelaide and many country towns, but is rarely seen in cultivation.

BEEFWOOD *G. striata* R.Br. is a much larger dry area tree usually **10–14 m high,** and widespread throughout the Inland in all States except Victoria and Tasmania. The **bark** is thick, rough, and furrowed and the foliage erect and rather leathery. Striate **leaves** are long, linear, and silky-hoary when young. Cream **inflorescences,** each about 5–7 cm long, are abundantly produced in slender racemes.

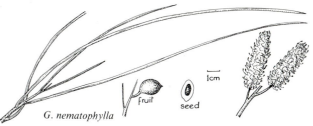
G. nematophylla
fruit   seed   1cm

FERN-LEAVED GREVILLEA, ABERGUBBER

Grevillea pteridifolia Knight   PROTEACEAE
(syn. *G. chrysodendron* R. Br.).

One of the loveliest flowering trees of northern Australia, "Fern-leaved Grevillea" is an inhabitant of the monsoonal areas, usually found along the edges of fresh water swamps or streams. It is fairly widespread throughout tropical Western Australia, the Northern Territory, and Queensland.

Only a small tree, **up to about 8 m high,** it usually has a single trunk, and spreading, rather erect branches. In some ways it resembles the "Silky Oak" (*G. robusta*) but is much smaller, and has a more open habit of growth..

The large fern-like foliage consists of pinnate leaves made up of long linear segments, 15–20 cm in length. Borne over a long period throughout the dry season, the **flowers** are spectacular. They are carried in large, terminal racemes of very showy, rich orange spikes or cones. They are full of **nectar** which is sometimes used by the Aborigines as nourishment.

Fruits or follicles are roundish in shape, and about 2 cm long.

A glorious sight in full flower, this tree is one of the very best tree grevilleas, and should be extensively cultivated, at least in tropical gardens where it is known to be very hardy. Little is known of its adaptability to the cooler climates of the south.

Several other species of *Grevillea* are noted for their similar and beautiful orange or flame-like flowers.

RUSH-LEAF GREVILLEA *G. juncifolia* Hook. is an inland tree, **up to 7 m high,** with much to commend it as an ornamental flowering tree for dry conditions. It has long, erect, needle-like **leaves,** and masses of orange-yellow **flowers** in spring.

FLAME GREVILLEA *G. eriostachya* Lindl. (syn. *G. excelsior* Diels.). Common in the southern sand plains of Western Australia, it is usually only a tall, very thin, pine-like shrub, or sometimes a tree growing **to 7 m.** From October to January the orange **flower spikes** are prolific and spectacular.

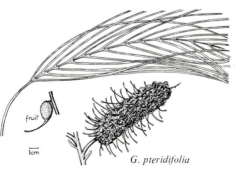

G. pteridifolia

SILKY OAK

Grevillea robusta A. Cunn. ex R. Br. PROTEACEAE

Well known both for ornament and timber, "Silky Oak" is an inhabitant of the rain forests extending from the Clarence River in New South Wales to Maryborough and inland to the Bunya Mountains in Queensland. Valued for its distinctive silky-textured timber, the tree has now become quite rare in its natural state.

However, it is frequently planted in streets, parks, and gardens, and is seen in many parts of Australia where frosts are not severe. At its best it is an erect, pyramidal tree, **30–40 m high,** with a dark brown or grey, rough-barked **trunk,** about 1 m in diameter. **Bark** is furrowed and fissured, with a corky outer layer. The graceful, fern-like foliage is made up of large, doubly pinnate **leaves,** the individual leaflets divided into narrow lobes. **Flowers** usually appear in early summer when they are borne in large, spectacular racemes of brush-like blooms, a bright cadmium yellow in colour. **Fruits** are boat-shaped follicles with a slender beak, about 2 cm long, and containing flat, oval-shaped **seeds.**

"Silky Oak" grows rapidly from seed, seldom exceeding **16 m in height** when cultivated. It forms a fine, ornamental specimen tree best suited to rich, moist soils in warm situations, but is adaptable.

WHITE SILKY OAK *G. hilliana* F. Muell,. is a somewhat smaller tree of the same areas but found as far north as Cairns in Queensland. It occasionally grows **to nearly 33 m** but is more usually only about half this height. This is also an upright forest tree with large glossy **leaves,** usually over 15 cm long, entire, or deeply lobed, with a silky white undersurface. The long, white **flower spikes** are borne in numerous axillary racemes. **Fruits** are egg-shaped follicles.

The **timber** of this tree is beautifully figured, hard, and heavy, and dresses and polishes well, resembling that of the "Scrub Beefwood" (see p. 214) in appearance. This too is an ornamental tree particularly suited to warm climates.

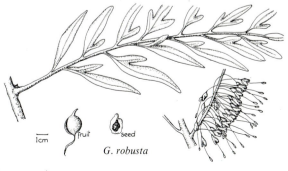

G. robusta

PIN CUSHION HAKEA

Hakea laurina R.Br. PROTEACEAE

Native only to parts of the south coast and some sand plain areas 160 km or so inland in Western Australia, "Pin Cushion Hakea" is seldom seen growing naturally, and where it is encountered it is usually only a slender shrub rarely reaching small tree size. It is better known in cultivation, where, under favourable conditions, it can form a dense, spreading tree **5–8 m high.** Even when it remains shrubby it is usually densely branched and rounded in habit.

The genus *Hakea* is limited to Australia, with more than one hundred species being found throughout the continent. These are all evergreens, mainly shrubs, though a few attain small tree proportions. They are distinguished by their hard woody **fruits,** each of which contains two black winged **seeds.** It is only these fruits that make it possible to identify some species from the genus, *Grevillea*, to which they are closely related.

"Pin Cushion Hakea" is much loved for its **flowers** which appear in autumn and winter. These are globular inflorescences, about the size of a golf ball, bright red or pink in colour, and covered with protruding cream styles like short pins. An all-red colour form also occurs. The flower buds are contained in bracts which peel off as the flower opens, each stage of opening being very beautiful, and adding interest to the overall effect.

The **leaves** resemble those of many of the eucalypt species but with prominent longitudinal or striate nerves. When making new growth the young tips are a lovely, silky, golden-bronze colour, and the old leaves assume bright colours prior to falling.

GRASS-LEAVED HAKEA *H. francisiana* F. Muell. is an inland species from South Australia and Western Australia favouring well-drained, sandy soils. A tall shrub or small tree **to 7 m** with upright foliage, it has long, narrow, striate **leaves,** and prominent clusters of pink, red, or cream **flower spikes** produced over a long period in late winter and spring, and often blooming twice in one season.

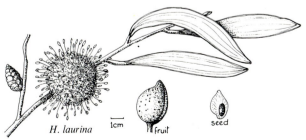
H. laurina   1cm   fruit   seed

CORK-BARK TREE

Hakea suberea S. Moore   PROTEACEAE
(*H. lorea* Black non R.Br.)

"Cork-Bark Tree," a rather grotesque but fascinating species, is native to arid central Australia where it is a conspicuous feature of the landscape. Usually twisted and contorted, often in fantastic attitudes, these trees command attention wherever they are seen. Resembling in some ways large bonsai trees, they have great appeal for both the tourist and the plant-lover.

At maturity, the tree is **only 5–8 m high,** with usually a rather sparse, but occasionally dense head of foliage. **Bark** is dark brown, very rough, and cork-like, and the **trunk** often thick and twisted. The **leaves** are terete, and up to 60 cm long, grey, or grey-green in colour, and usually covered with a whitish tomentum.

The **flowers** are in large, torch-like spikes, cream or yellow in colour, and sweetly scented. They are loaded with **honey** which is much relished by the Aborigines of these areas. An old tree in full flower is a wonderful sight.

At all times the "Cork-Bark Tree" has an attraction all of its own, its ancient appearance suggesting hardiness and longevity.

SMALL-LEAVED CORK-BARK *H. divaricata* Johnson (*H. intermedia* Ewart & Davies). This species is similar in appearance to "Cork-Bark Tree" but has a denser crown of foliage which is not covered with a whitish-grey tomentum. The **leaves** are short and divided, an olive-green in colour. **Flowers** are similar but greenish. This tree is often found growing in association with *H. suberea*, but it has a less grotesque habit. It is fairly widespread throughout central Australia.

NEEDLE HAKEA *H. leucoptera* R.Br. is another dry area species from south and eastern Australia which reaches small tree proportions. The long, pungent, needle-like **leaves** are an attractive hoary grey, and the **inflorescences** white, borne in axillary racemes.

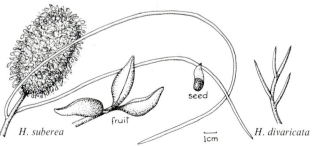

H. suberea   fruit   seed   1cm   *H. divaricata*

TULIPWOOD

Harpullia pendula Planch. ex F. Muell.   SAPINDACEAE

"Tulipwood" is a dense, evergreen tree from the coastal scrubs of northern New South Wales and Queensland as far north as Cairns, often found in sandy soils near the sea.

It is fairly extensively cultivated, particularly as a street tree in the warm, sub-tropical to tropical climates of many Queensland cities, and to a lesser extent in New South Wales. The tree grows quite well as far south as Adelaide but is rarely seen in plantings in that city.

In its natural forest environment "Tulipwood" reaches a **height of 28 m,** with a trunk 60 cm in diameter, sometimes buttressed at the base. When cultivated it is much shorter and more spreading, with a dense, shapely crown, and smooth grey **bark** which is shed in flakes. **Leaves** are alternate, and pinnate, consisting of 3–8 glossy, bright green leaflets, narrowly elliptical in shape. The young shoots are downy, and an attractive reddish-brown in colour.

The **flowers** which are borne in narrow panicles in the leaf axils are comparatively inconspicuous, but are followed by bright orange **fruits** which are the colourful feature of the tree. These split open to reveal one or two, jet black, shiny, round **seeds,** providing a pleasing contrast to the orange fruits. The fruits are variable both in the time of cropping, and the quantity produced. A tree that bears well is a beautiful sight.

"Tulipwood" is a shapely evergreen with handsome foliage, that makes it particularly suitable for ornamental planting. It is well suited to street planting as it is relatively pest-free, and does not produce troublesome roots. In addition, the tree's natural habit of growth produces many twiggy small branchlets which make it easy to control with regular, light pruning.

It prefers rich, moist soils, and is fairly slow growing, at least when planted in climates cooler than its natural environment.

The heavy, close-grained, dark brown and yellow **timber** is attractive and useful, but is no longer very plentiful.

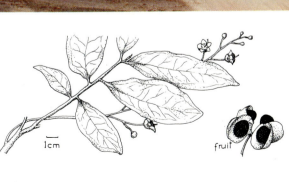

BULLOCK BUSH, ROSEWOOD
Heterodendrum oleaefolium Desf. SAPINDACEAE

A very widespread species from the dry parts of temperate Australia, "Bullock Bush" can be seen growing in many varying situations from sand dunes to deep soil areas, and from rocky slope to open plain country. It is a small tree native to all States except Tasmania.

The conspicuous feature of this tree is its blue-green to silvery-grey foliage, and often contorted habit of growth which adds to its attractiveness in the landscape. **Seldom more than 5–7 m high** it can be a single or multi-stemmed tree with several joined and crooked, thick main stems. The rough **bark** on the **trunk** and branches is thick, dark brown, and deeply fissured. In appearance it closely resembles the bark of two frequently associated trees, "Sugarwood" (*Myoporum platycarpum*) and "Long-leaved Emu Bush" (*Eremophila longifolia*).

The tree is heavily canopied with olive-like **leaves,** 5–10 cm long, and covered with an adpressed hoariness, which gives it its characteristic, greyish appearance. **Flowers** are small, somewhat bell-shaped without petals, green or yellow in colour, and carried in short, dense panicles in summer. The peculiar **fruits** are made up of 1–4 globular lobes, each containing one black shiny **seed.**

Timber is hard and dark brown but of no special importance.

The foliage is valued as cattle fodder, and this is probably the reason why the tree is on the list of South Australia's protected plants. Even so, stock are sometimes poisoned by eating the foliage of "Bullock Bush," usually from young plants, and care should be taken to supplement it with other feed.

Good specimens of this tree are ornamental, and it can easily be pruned to produce a shapely, effective, shade and shelter tree. Occasionally one sees "Bullock Bush" resembling a dwarf bonsai tree, and it is then that the attraction of this often overlooked plant is fully appreciated.

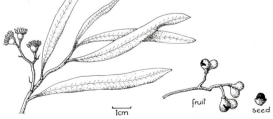

NATIVE FRANGIPANI

Hymenosporum flavum F. Muell. PITTOSPORACEAE

"Native Frangipani" is the only Australian species of *Hymenosporum*, and is closely related to the *Pittosporum* genus, which it resembles in certain respects. It is native to the coastal brush forests of eastern Australia, extending from the Hunter River in New South Wales to Atherton in Queensland.

In tropical Queensland some trees grow **to 25 m** with a stem diameter of 30 cm or more, but further south it is much smaller. In cultivation it is usually only a small, very slender and upright tree **up to 10 m high. Bark** is grey and roughish, and the **branches** sparse, radiating in whorls from the main stem. The deep lustrous green **leaves,** which resemble those of the *Pittosporum*, are alternately grouped at the ends of the twiggy branchlets, oval-oblong in shape, and 7–15 cm long. This is a very fine flowering tree, that begins to bloom in early spring when the fragrant, open, tubular **flowers** are cream coloured. They darken with age to a deep sulphur yellow before they drop. The effect of masses of cream and yellow flowers is very lovely. Flowering period extends to early summer. The 4 cm diameter flowers in terminal corymbs are sweetly scented, and about the size and shape of those of the "Frangipani," from which the common name is derived. In other respects the tree bears no resemblance to the "Frangipani" at all.

Fruit capsules are hard and brown, containing numerous, closely packed layers of brown, papery **seeds** which germinate freely.

"Native Frangipani" is a quick-growing, free-flowering, small evergreen, which is easily cultivated, but requires copious watering, especially in the early stages. It is not particular as to soils, and grows quite successfully in the cooler, temperate climates of Melbourne and Adelaide, though it resents frosty conditions. In cool climates it is not recommended as a lawn specimen, because of its habit of continuously dropping leaves, and its susceptibility to the effects of strong winds. It is best planted among other trees where it can receive their protection, and its slender growth harmonizes well with group or clump planting.

BLACK GIN

Kingia australis R.Br.　　　　　　　　　　　　　　　　LILIACEAE

"Black Gin" belongs to the same family as the better known "Grass Trees" (*Xanthorrhoea*), but is distinguished by its many drumstick-like heads of flowers which are quite different from the solitary tall flower spikes of the "Grass Tree."

It is found only in Western Australia, being native to the higher rainfall south-west, and growing usually in sandy, gravelly, or rocky soils. Here it is sometimes seen in groups among "Karri" and "Jarrah" trees, or as a lone sentinel on rocky outcrops in the Stirling Range and elsewhere. Wherever they occur, these magnificent and unique plants have rare beauty and great character.

The **trunk** is black, **up to 3 m or more high** with a tufted head of rush-like **leaves,** the older ones reflexed or drooping. These are often crowned with a ring of flower or seed heads, like drumsticks, about 30 cm in length. The **flowers** are creamy white, and the **seeds** black.

They are long lived and extremely slow in growth, taking many, many years to attain their characteristic appearance. It is this slowness of growth which has curtailed the planting of "Black Gin" in gardens, a purpose for which it is unsurpassed as a structural plant.

GRASS TREES, BLACK BOYS *Xanthorrhoea* species. These, too, are beautiful plants which are uniquely Australian. They are closely related to the "Black Gin" but much more common, some twelve or more species being found throughout different parts of temperate Australia. These are often stemless bushes, but in some species eventually form small trees with a thick, rough stem and tufted canopy of sharp, hard, rush-like **leaves.** The elongated spikes of creamy-white **flowers** bloom irregularly, and are held high above the foliage on a long, smooth stalk in spear-like fashion. These are followed by sharp, protruding **seed capsules** which transform the flower head into something resembling an ancient spiked club.

"Grass Trees" are also very long lived and slow growing. It is a tragedy to see fine mature plants being destroyed in new housing estates, where they could, if they were preserved, become unique and trouble-free assets to the garden.

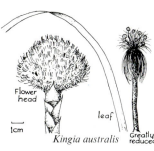

Flower head
1cm
Kingia australis
leaf
Greatly reduced

Xanthorrhoea sp.
Greatly reduced

PYRAMID TREE, NORFOLK ISLAND HIBISCUS
Lagunaria patersonii G. Don. MALVACEAE

"Pyramid Tree" is the solitary species of the genus, *Lagunaria*, and belongs to the "Mallow" family which includes such well-known genera as *Hibiscus*, *Abutilon*, etc.

Native to coastal Queensland as well as to Norfolk Island, it is a very ornamental and useful tree, which has long been in cultivation in Australia, as well as overseas.

The tree usually grows erect and pyramidal, with a dense, low-branching crown, and little spread. **Height** varies according to conditions but seldom exceeds **10–14 m. Bark** is rough, dark grey, and shallowly fissured. **Leaves** are oval shaped, rather rough in texture, dull green with a whitish, scurfy undersurface. The new leaves are much paler, providing a pleasing contrast.

Occurring singly in the leaf axils, the flower buds are small and conical. They open to reveal handsome, rose-pink, Hibiscus-like **blossoms,** 3–5 cm across with 5 velvety textured, recurved petals. They flower over a long period during the warm months of spring, summer, and early autumn. The hard, egg-shaped **fruits** that follow are a pale greyish-green with a rough velvety texture, and are rather like flower buds at first. They eventually turn dry at maturity, opening to reveal 5 valves containing the **seeds.** These valves are lined with a mat of fine hairs. The irritating effect these have on the skin when handled has caused the tree to be called "Cow-itch Tree."

Lagunaria is successfully grown throughout Australia, particularly near the sea, where it has proved that it can withstand cold, salt-laden winds without visible "burning off." Tolerant of most soils including almost solid limestone, it is often used for planting on inland properties, but is not drought resistant.

Easily raised from seed, it grows rapidly, but requires some protection from extreme cold during its early years.

COASTAL TEA-TREE

Leptospermum laevigatum F. Muell.   MYRTACEAE

"Coastal Tea-Tree" is a useful but often neglected small tree inhabiting mainly the sand dunes and coastline of eastern and south-eastern Australia. It is occasionally found inland on sandy soils.

The genus *Leptospermum* consists mainly of shrubby species, some of which are the parents of garden hybrids now popularly cultivated, and valued for the beauty of their white, pink, or red flowers. Of the fifty recorded species, only three are not Australian.

The "Coastal Tea-Tree" is often found in harsh, wind-swept, coastal situations where it assumes leaning or crooked, but attractive attitudes. Often under these conditions it only grows to about 1 m in height, but under better situations forms a handsome tree **up to 10 m high** with a broad head of grey or blue-green, often drooping foliage. The thick **trunk** and **branches** are covered with layers of loose, flaky **bark,** grey, or light brown in colour.

Leaves are 1–2 cm long by about 50 mm wide. It was the leaves of another species (*L. scoparium*) which Captain Cook and his crew used to brew tea, thus giving the name "Tea-Tree" to the genus.

The **flowers** are produced freely in spring and summer. These are white, open, 5-petalled, and about 2 cm across. The **fruits** are small woody capsules containing numerous tiny **seeds.**

"Coastal Tea-Tree" is a particularly useful tree for harsh, seaside conditions, both as a sand binder or as an ornamental specimen. It is also frequently used as a hedge or to produce a hedge-row effect; it can form a very satisfactory windbreak against burning, salt-laden winds which spell death to so many weaker plants. This tree will tolerate most soil conditions and it could well be considered as a garden subject in better areas where its flowers and informal habit would be better displayed. It is also a fine **honey** tree for apiarists.

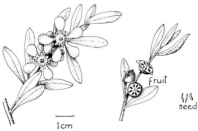

RED-LEAVED PALM

Livistona mariae F. Muell.　　　　　　　　　　　　　　　PALMAE

There are several species of Palms native to Australia, but perhaps the "Red-leaved Palm" is the most interesting, owing to its unique and isolated habitat. This tree occurs only in the Finke Gorge, popularly known as Palm Valley—a deep and beautiful, red, rocky gorge. It is situated about 150 km south-west of Alice Springs and has become one of the main tourist attractions of central Australia.

The palms grow only in deep, sandy soil in the base of the valley, often in company with "River Red Gum."

The palm itself is very stately in appearance, growing very slowly to **14–20 m in height.** During the earlier years the young fronds are reddish coloured, a feature which gives the tree the common name, "Red-leaved Palm." The **trunk** is slender and upright, topped with a broad head of cabbage-palm **leaves.** They often rise out of fairly heavy undershrubs, giving the Palm Valley area a truly tropical appearance, which contrasts strangely with the surrounding arid countryside.

The creamy **flowers** are borne in dense panicles, and the **fruits** that follow are dark brown when ripe. **Seeds** are the size of small marbles, and are abundantly produced, thus providing, in favourable seasons, a ready means of regeneration of this unique species.

Seen naturally against a red rocky background this stately palm is one of Australia's most interesting and beautiful trees, and is one of the rarest palms in the world.

It has been grown from seeds as far south as Adelaide, where growth is very slow, but it warrants greater attention as a garden subject, particularly in warm sub-tropical areas.

There are three other species of *Livistona* native to Australia.

CABBAGE TREE PALM *L. australis* Mart. is a tall and slender tree **up to 28 m high,** found fairly commonly on the east coast, extending from Queensland to Gippsland in Victoria.

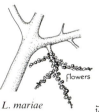

L. mariae — flowers — 1cm

Leaf stem

seed
fruit

QUEENSLAND NUT, POPPEL NUT
Macadamia integrifolia Maid. & Betche.   PROTEACEAE

"Queensland Nut" is a rain forest tree of the eastern coastal scrubs from just south of Sydney to Maryborough in Queensland.

Its delicious edible nuts give it considerable economic importance. Overseas, particularly in Hawaii and California, its cultivation has become an important primary industry. In these countries improved strains have been developed from which quality thin-shelled nuts are harvested.

From seed the tree usually takes about 6–7 years to bear, but as the fruit of seedlings is unreliable, new plants should be vegetatively propagated from a good nut-bearing tree.

Under natural conditions it reaches a **height of 20 m** but seldom attains more than half this size when cultivated. The tree is very **densely branched** with dark green glossy **leaves,** and a slightly rough, brown **bark.** The **leaves** are very variable, 7–22 cm long, usually in whorls of three. They can be entire, or divided, sometimes wavy, or harshly serrated with small, pungent teeth. New shoots are an attractive bronze or pink colour. The small creamish or pale brown **flowers** in long, pendulous, catkin-like racemes appear in profusion in spring, when they provide a pleasing contrast to the dark foliage.

The rounded **fruits** (follicles) are in clusters, and coated with a soft green covering enclosing the hard-shelled brown nut. The oil-rich kernel, when toasted or salted, has a very pleasing flavour.

This is a worthwhile tree for garden culture, being ornamental as well as useful. It is slow growing in cultivation but eventually makes a permanent tree. *Macadamia* can be grown in cooler climates, but prefers rich, moist soils and copious summer watering in its early stages.

SMALL-FRUITED QUEENSLAND NUT *M. ternifolia* F. Muell. syn. minor F. M. Bailey is a Queensland species which is cultivated, and requires similar growing conditions to "Queensland Nut." It is of similar appearance but much smaller in stature, sometimes only shrubby.

BALL NUT *M. praealta* F. M. Bailey is also very similar and inhabits the same regions, but has a different **leaf** and **flower** arrangement, as well as larger non-edible **fruits** about the size of a golf ball.

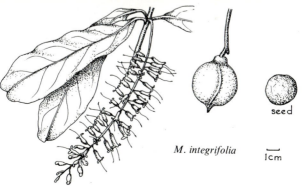

M. integrifolia   1cm

INLAND PAPERBARK

Melaleuca glomerata F. Muell.   MYRTACEAE

"Inland Paperbark" is a small, somewhat spreading and low-branched tree up **to 10 m high,** inhabiting inland creeks and dry streams. It is found from the Flinders Ranges in South Australia northwards to central Australia, and in Western Australia and western New South Wales.

"Paperbarks" or "Tea-trees" (the accepted common name of the leptospermums) belong to the large genus, *Melaleuca*, and are sometimes called "Honey Myrtles," particularly the shrubby species, of which there are over a hundred native to Australia.

The term "Paperbark" is very appropriate, particularly to the trees of the genus, many of which possess a papery deciduous **bark** that hangs loosely in layers on the **trunk** and **branches,** in some species, grey or creamy coloured, or a very vivid white in others.

They are distinguished botanically by the stalkless (sessile) **flowers** which are clustered in cylindrical spikes often like small bottlebrushes; each flower comprises very small petals but with many long stamens united into five bundles. The **fruits** are also sessile, small, and woody, and cluster along the branches, growing a little larger each year they remain on the plant. Each **seed capsule** contains numerous tiny **seeds** which are released after picking or fire.

Melaleucas are often the characteristic tree of swampy, poorly drained brackish soils, and are sometimes found in pure stands along the banks of streams and estuaries or lagoons where their roots are immersed in water. This is not always the case, however, as some are native to the dry regions.

Melaleuca glomerata is one such species, and is found growing in sandy soils along the dried up waterways of the inland.

It is a handsome tree, sometimes only a shrub, well suited, where conditions are favourable, to ornamental planting. Its low spreading **branches** afford good shade and shelter for stock. The **bark** is white and papery, and the **leaves** grey coloured, small, and very narrow, acutely pointed. The globular **flowers** occur in dense terminal heads, white, or creamy yellow in colour, and make a fine display over the whole tree during late spring.

flower fruit
1cm

WHITE PAPERBARK
Melaleuca cuticularis Labill.　　　　　　　　　MYRTACEAE

Very few of the many melaleucas native to the higher rainfall South West of Western Australia reach tree proportions. "White Paperbark" is an exception, and is one of the larger "Paperbarks" of these swamplands where in certain parts it is the dominant tree of the area. In places near Denmark it can be seen as the only tree in water-logged pastures where it has been allowed to remain as shelter for stock. It is only found in the wet swamps in and near the "Karri" country.

Where it still remains in natural thickets the tree is usually spindly, crooked and small, but it is seen at its best where single specimens remain in cleared land. Under these conditions **the tree reaches 12–16 m in height** with a rather stout trunk surmounted by a dense canopy of dark green foliage.

The main feature is its **gleaming white papery bark** on trunk and branches, outstanding even in a genus noted for this feature. The narrow **leaves,** arranged in opposite pairs, are small, up to 1 cm long, glabrous, and sharply pointed. The small, white **flowers** which occur from June to November are in small terminal heads of one to three, but are not prolific. At its best, this beautiful tree is well worthy of cultivation.

M. cymbifolia Benth., a closely related small tree of the same regions, lacks the vivid white bark and has smaller, softer **leaves.**

SWAMP PAPERBARK *Melaleuca rhaphiophylla* Schau. is perhaps the largest of the western "Paperbarks." It inhabits sandy swamplands in the Perth district extending north as far as the Murchison River and south to the "Karri" forests, sometimes in association with *M. preissiana*.

It is a small to medium-sized tree, **up to 14 m high,** with a rather short, thick trunk (about 1 m in diameter), and branches clothed in grey and white papery bark. The tree is usually crooked or leaning with gnarled and twisted branches. More mature specimens have a look of very great age about them. **Foliage** is a very dark green, the **leaves** are 1–2 cm long, and very narrow, recurved, and sharply pointed. The **flowers** are white in terminal, rather loose spikes, and bloom in spring.

This is a useful tree for water-logged coastal sandy soils.

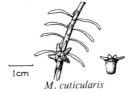

M. rhaphiophylla   1cm   *M. cuticularis*

KANGAROO TEA-TREE, SOUTH AUSTRALIAN PAPERBARK

Melaleuca halmaturorum F. Muell.   MYRTACEAE

"Kangaroo Tea-Tree" is a common small straggling tree of the swampy, salty soils of many parts of the South Australian coastline, especially the Coorong and the South-East, and extending into western Victoria. It is also found on Kangaroo Island and occasionally inland in South Australia around the edges of salt lagoons.

Several of the many "Paperbarks" found in the coastal swamps of the eastern States and Western Australia are described in the following pages; but this particular species is the only "Paperbark" tree found along the South Australian coastline. Its roots are often immersed in brackish water. "Moonah" (*M. lanceolata*) is also found in these parts but this is a rough-barked tree.

"Kangaroo Tea-Tree" is a short, crooked, straggling tree **up to 8 m high,** sometimes forming almost grotesque shapes, resembling an enlarged specimen of Japanese bonsai. Its irregular shape is enhanced by the low-branched, crooked, but rather erect **limbs** and thick papery white or grey deciduous **bark** which hangs in loose flakes from the trunk and branches. The **trunk** is short and thick, buttressed at the base by horizontally spreading roots which are partly visible above the ground.

The foliage forms a rather dense canopy at the ends of the branches. The small dark green crowded **leaves** are glabrous, small, and narrow, slightly curved, and decussate. The **flowers** are white and occur in terminal heads, usually in late spring.

This tree is particularly useful for planting in difficult, salty, poorly drained soils, and attempts should be made to re-establish it along the edges of streams and lakes where it was once the dominant tree. The Patawalonga River at Glenelg, an Adelaide beach suburb, is an example of an area where this tree once grew profusely and where it could be profitably re-established.

1cm

MOONAH, BLACK TEA-TREE

Melaleuca lanceolata Otto MYRTACEAE
(syn. *M. pubescens* Schau.).

"Moonah" was until recently, botanically known as *M. pubescens*, and this name is still commonly accepted. It is a small tree found throughout most of temperate Australia in open country in both coastal and inland situations often on poor limy soils, but almost always in areas exceeding a 300 mm rainfall. It avoids the wetter, mountainous regions.

The tree is found in all States except the Northern Territory and Tasmania. In Western Australia it inhabits the drier coastal regions of the south, and is sometimes confused with a very similar tree, *M. preissiana*, found in the wetter South-West regions.

A bushy small tree, **up to about 10 m high,** it is distinguished by its very dark green almost black foliage and rough, dark-grey **bark** which combine to give it quite a sombre, but characteristic, appearance when not in flower. The crown is rounded, very dense and low-branched, the **small twigs** whitish. **Leaves** are small, narrow and crowded, rather thick and curved, with sharp points. The young growth is a much brighter green than the mature foliage. The **flowers** occur in loose fluffy cylindrical spikes at irregular periods, but the tree blooms profusely in summer when the massed display of white blossom against the dark foliage is a very rewarding sight.

"Moonah" is a useful windbreak tree for inland plantings on poor alkaline soils, or as a specimen tree for coastal or seaside situations where more favoured plants are difficult to grow. It is a wind-resistant tree that will grow on almost any soil, and also a good honey tree, although the quality of the **honey** is not first rate.

Melaleuca preissiana Schau. from Western Australia is most easily distinguished from "Moonah" by its papery **bark** and its preference for coastal swampy situations, although there are slight botanical differences in the small erect **leaves, flowers,** and rather broader **fruits.**

M. parviflora Lindl. is sometimes listed as a Western Australian species, but it is possibly the same species as the preceding paperbark.

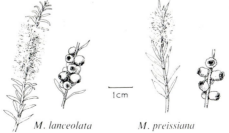

M. lanceolata   *M. preissiana*

WHITE TREE, CAJUPUT TREE, PUNK TREE
Melaleuca leucadendra L.   MYRTACEAE

The tree bearing this name was the original species on which the genus *Melaleuca* was founded, having been discovered in Ambon in Indonesia, and later, by Linnaeus in India. At this time the oil in the leaves was known as "Oil of Cajuput," the tree then bearing the botanical name of Cajuput. It is ironical that the genus was founded from a species outside Australia, since more than a hundred species are endemic to this country, and only eight have been recorded elsewhere.

All literature on this tree indicates that it belongs to a closely related but botanically confused group of "Paperbarks." These are trees of the coastal swamps and lagoons extending from just south of Sydney to the tropical north of Australia, and thence to Indonesia and Malaysia. C. N. Debenham, in the March 1963 issue of *Australian Plants*, gives "White Tree" as the common name of *M. leucadendra*, and the "Cajuput Tree" as *M. cajuputii* Powell. Other names, for closely allied species, are *M. quinquenervia* S. T. Blake, "Broad-leaved Paperbark," which is common in the southern extremities of the above range; *M. viridiflora* Sol. ex Gaertn. and several others.

All are very beautiful trees, similar in appearance, and favouring similar conditions.

M. leucadendra is a tree **up to 20 m high,** with layers of papery white bark and often a fairly straight **trunk.** Like many swamp dwellers the roots at the base are partly above ground level, partly immersed in water. The **leaves** are larger than is the case with most of the genus, broadly lanceolate, 5–8 cm long, rather rigid and prominently veined, and a dull or silvery green in colour. The small bottlebrush-like **flowers** make a massed display in spring. These are usually cream, but mauve, pink, or red flowers occur in some trees. They are laden with **honey** and useful to beekeepers.

The **bark** is sometimes used for lining fern baskets, and the oil of the leaves has medicinal value.

This is an extremely ornamental tree, and one of the few suited to brackish water-logged conditions exposed to strong winds. It is cultivated successfully as far south as Adelaide, although it is probable that many of the trees grown under this name are others of the group, such as those mentioned in the text above.

M. leucadendra

stamens

1cm

NARROW-LEAF PAPERBARK
Melaleuca linariifolia Sm. MYRTACEAE

One of the many paperbarks found along the coastal estuaries and streams from southern New South Wales to Cape Melville in Queensland, this particular species occurs from about Jervis Bay in the south to Gladstone in Queensland. It is a very beautiful tree, **7–14 m high,** with a white papery **bark** and rather thick **trunk** buttressed with horizontally spreading roots visible slightly above ground level. The crown is usually bushy with bright green, or bluish-green, soft foliage. The **leaves** are 3 cm or more long and narrow, arranged in opposite pairs on the branches.

Flowering is prolific, so that the whole tree appears to be covered with snow. The fluffy white **flowers** occur in loose bundles held prominently above the foliage, the new growth continuing during the flowering period. The main flowering period is in November.

A valuable ornamental and possibly street tree in reasonably wet districts, it prefers non-alkaline soils and is sometimes difficult to establish.

M. trichostachya Lindl. is similar and closely related. It is of wide distribution extending from the north-east coast across the Great Dividing Range to many parts of inland Queensland and the Northern Territory where it follows dry sandy streams, but retains a constant character throughout. *M. alternifolia* Cheel is a smaller but closely related tree with narrower leaves. It has a more restricted range, being found mainly between the Stroud and Richmond rivers in New South Wales. *M. dissitiflora* F. Muell. from the Flinders Ranges in South Australia is another very similar species. The **leaves** of all species are rich in oils.

PRICKLY-LEAF PAPERBARK *M. styphelioides* Sm. is another beautiful paperbark of the coastal division of New South Wales and southern Queensland. Although different botanically, it is mentioned because it is commonly cultivated. It frequently reaches **20 m in height** with small, broad, prickly **leaves** and masses of small cream **flower spikes** in late spring. This useful tree grows on most soils, even those which are poorly drained and brackish. The **timber** of all species is very durable in damp ground or wet conditions.

M. linariifolia

1cm

M. styphelioides

WHITE CEDAR, BEAD TREE

Melia azedarach L. var. *australasica* C.DC.   MELIACEAE

One of the few Australian deciduous trees, "White Cedar" inhabits the brush forests of the east coast, extending from the Illawarra districts in New South Wales north to the coastal brush forests of Queensland. It is also native to India, Indonesia, and New Guinea.

The tree grows naturally very tall and long-stemmed in its forest environment, but when cultivated has a much shorter and more spreading appearance, seldom exceeding **10–15 m in height.**

Once frequently planted as a park, garden, or street tree, it has since been found to have a root system unsuitable for footpaths. This and the untidy dropping of the ripe fruits have caused it to fall from favour. Often, existing trees have been mutilated by constant and severe pruning. Left untouched, however, this can be a very lovely tree with an appealing, wide, almost horizontal, branching habit, providing good shade in summer. Being deciduous it does not block the sunlight in winter.

The foliage is a handsome bright glossy green, the alternate, compound leaves usually bipinnate, with numerous leaflets.

Individual **leaflets** are ovate and prominently toothed on the margins. The lilac **flowers** are fragrant and appear in erect terminal panicles that are prolific in spring. The **fruits,** which are in clusters, are oval to round, bead-like drupes with a hard bony stone. They are pale green in colour, but ripen to a yellowish-brown, and remain on the tree long after the leaves have fallen. **Bark** is grey and slightly furrowed, and the **timber** light, open grained, and useful for interior woodwork.

Despite its tropical habitat, "White Cedar" is an extremely adaptable tree that can be easily grown in most soils and situations in a rainfall as low as 300–400 mm.

SUGARWOOD

Myoporum platycarpum R.Br.   MYOPORACEAE

"Sugarwood" is a widespread tree found growing in the drier parts of temperate Australia often in poor, limy soils. It is seldom seen in colonies, but is usually scattered over large areas as isolated specimens or in small groups, particularly in open, flat country.

The genus *Myoporum* consists of about twenty species, most of them Australian. These vary from prostrate ground cover plants to small trees up to about **10 m high.**

The name "Sugarwood" was given to this particular species because of the sweet resin which it sometimes exudes. This resin was used by the Aborigines as an adhesive cement.

The trees, when young, are quite tidy and symmetrical, although they are usually seen as sturdy old specimens of great character with many gnarled and dead limbs, but with upright **trunks** covered with very rough, dark, flaky **bark.** On drooping **branchlets,** the **leaves,** about 5 cm long, are a pale, shiny green, narrow but fleshy, with a few small teeth on the upper part. They contrast well with the dark bark. The small starry, white or pinkish **flowers** are abundantly produced in dense clusters from August to December. **Fruits** are small, rather fleshy drupes, each of which contains 2 seeds.

The soft, yellow **timber** is fragrantly scented. For this reason the tree is sometimes wrongly called "Sandalwood."

This is a useful fodder tree and an important species in dry inland situations. It is a protected plant in South Australia.

BOOBIALLA *M. insulare* R. Br. is a much used species, native to all States except Queensland and the Northern Territory. A densely foliaged evergreen growing **up to 10 m** or **sometimes a shrub,** it is wind and fire resistant and often used for dense shelter belts around farm houses. This species is also useful for coastal planting as it withstands salt winds very well.

The rather large, somewhat fleshy **leaves** are a bright shiny green, and the starry, white **flowers** are followed by fleshy purplish **fruits** or berries. It flowers for most of the year.

All the myoporums are easily grown in most soils.

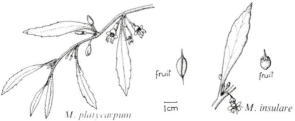

M. platycarpum   fruit   1cm   fruit   *M. insulare*

ANTARCTIC BEECH, TASMANIAN MYRTLE

Nothofagus cunninghamii Oerst. FAGACEAE

The genus *Nothofagus*, in Australia, consists of four species. It is the country's representative of the European "Beech Trees" (*Fagus*), which are deciduous but otherwise very similar in general appearance.

"Antarctic Beech" is a large, often spreading, evergreen tree, found in moist, rich, mountain valleys of parts of Victoria and Tasmania. Once commonly encountered in the Otway Ranges, Baw Baw Mountains, and upper Yarra districts in Victoria, it has been so often destroyed by fire and by man that it is now quite rare in these areas. It is common in Tasmania where it is known as "Tasmanian Myrtle".

At its robust best, the tree reaches heights **exceeding 33 m,** with a **trunk** large in girth, and covered with thick, rough **bark.** It is often seen with more than one main stem joined at the base, a feature which sometimes adds to its characteristically handsome appearance under natural conditions.

The foliage is deep green and dense, the **leaves** roundish in shape, 6–12 mm long, with rather wavy, toothed margins, and arranged in fan-like sprays. In early spring the young foliage is a rich bronze colour, and strikingly beautiful. **Flowers** are small and catkin-like; the male flowers are produced low down on the stem; the female flowers occur in threes on the upper part. **Fruits** are produced usually in threes, and contain winged **seeds** which are seldom viable after about 12 months. Regeneration from seed is very slow.

Timber is soft and reddish coloured, polishes and dresses well, and has been used in joinery work.

NEGROHEAD BEECH *N. moorei* Maid., sometimes called "Antarctic Beech," is a very similar, closely related large tree native to the high altitudes of the MacPherson Range in Queensland, and the mountain slopes of coastal New South Wales. This lovely tree is readily distinguished by its similarly shaped but larger **leaves** which are 4–5 cm long.

TANGLEFOOT *N. gunnii* Hook. is a truly deciduous species from alpine Tasmania. It is a straggly shrub or small tree whose **leaves** turn bright yellow in the autumn.

N. cunninghamii

fruit seed male flower

N. moorei

WESTERN AUSTRALIAN CHRISTMAS TREE
Nuytsia floribunda R.Br. LORANTHACEAE

Native only to Western Australia, "Christmas Tree" is one of Australia's most remarkable trees, and indeed, would rank as one of the finest flowering trees on earth.

It is a member of the well-known "Mistletoe" family which consists mostly of semi-parasitic shrubs growing on the branches of host trees. "Christmas Tree" differs in that it forms a tree with roots in the soil which depend partly on the roots of other plants for their nourishment.

The tree has quite an extensive habitat range from the Murchison River in the north to Israelite Bay on the south coast, and extending in places some 300 km inland. Rainfall is in the 350–1100 mm range, and soils always sandy, peaty, or of granite origin.

It is not a graceful tree, often possessing a very thick rough-barked **trunk,** stiff upright **branches,** and rather heavy looking foliage. The **timber** is very soft and weak, and the tree is unsafe to climb even by children. **Leaves** are narrow, pointed, and of thick texture.

"Christmas Tree" begins to flower in October but reaches its full brilliance round about Christmas time. **Flowers** are so abundant at this time that the whole tree becomes a glowing mass of golden-orange. This tree in full bloom against a blue summer sky is a never-to-be-forgotten sight.

The tree is remarkable in that the **seeds** germinate to produce 3–6 cotyledons (seed leaves) instead of the normal two.

This is an exceptional tree which fortunately seems destined to remain in the Western Australian landscape for many years to come. Farmers have recognized that it is unique and worth preserving, and it can be seen left in paddocks (completely denuded of other tree cover) apparently feeding off the roots of grasses. It cannot be destroyed by fire and recovers by vigorous suckering, blooming even better than before.

Many attempts have been made by enthusiasts to grow this tree, but there is little evidence to date that it can be cultivated.

Photograph courtesy G. Watton

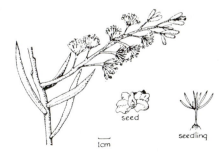

SCREW PINE, SCREW PALM

Pandanus spiralis R.Br.　　　　　　　　　　　　PANDANACEAE

Pandanus is a genus of plants from tropical and sub-tropical areas of the world. In Australia there are approximately twelve species, all of which are found in the northern half of the continent. The "Screw Pines" in Australia are not well known, and studies of native species are still being made.

Pandanus spiralis is one of the most widespread in Australia and spreads from the Kimberley district in Western Australia, across the Northern Territory to Cape York Peninsula. It favours swampy localities which are usually flooded during the wet season, and is often found along the edges of streams and lagoons. A waterlily lagoon with a background grouping of "Screw Pines" is a wonderful sight indeed.

The trees grow **to about 5–7 m in height,** with heads of long, narrow **leaves,** 1–2 m long, and arranged in spiral fashion. The edges of the leaves are armed with sharp teeth or spines. **Flowers** are small and produced in dense clusters which eventually develop into large pineapple-like **fruit,** sometimes reddish in colour. When ripe these break up into segments, which release the **seed,** and fall to the ground.

Many *Pandanus* have prop-like roots which grow from the main trunk into the ground forming extra supports. *P. spiralis*, however, has no such supports and is easily distinguished by their absence.

Fibre from the leaves has been used for sack-making, while Aborigines have used parts of the fruit for food.

Other "Screw Pines" in Australia include *P. aquaticus* F. Muell. which is found along watercourses; *P. basedowii* C. H. Wright which inhabits rocky cliffs in Arnhem Land; and *P. pedunculatus* R. Br. which is an east coast species from Queensland and New South Wales where it can be seen growing almost to the water's edge at beaches in these areas.

P. spiralis

P. pedunculatus

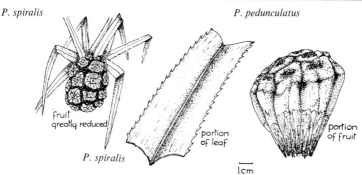

fruit greatly reduced

P. spiralis

portion of leaf

portion of fruit

1cm

NATIVE APRICOT, BERRIGAN
Pittosporum phylliraeoides DC. PITTOSPORACEAE

"Native Apricot" is a dry area species of an otherwise sub-tropical to tropical genus in Australia. *Pittosporum* is a large genus of evergreen plants, well represented both in Australia and New Zealand, and belonging to the family, Pittosporaceae, of which all other members are entirely Australian. The name is derived from the sticky pulp surrounding the seeds.

"Native Apricot" is found in areas of extremely dry to moderate rainfall throughout temperate Australia. On the fringe of the vast Nullarbor Plain tree life gradually gives way to "Blue-Bush" and grasses, but among this vegetation "Native Apricot" can be seen persisting as isolated stunted specimens for many kilometres, and with "Miljee" (*Acacia oswaldii*) are the last remaining plants of any height in this very arid terrain.

In the better parts of its range it grows into a very handsome, graceful tree, **7–14 m high.** It is easily recognized by its long, very slender, but sparse, weeping **branches** which often droop to near ground level, its bright green foliage, and its pale grey, smoothish **trunk.** These conspicuous features are unmistakable when it is seen among its dry area companions.

The bright green, glabrous **leaves** are 5–10 cm long by about 6–10 mm wide, with a small, hooked point. **Flowers** are small and bell-shaped, pale yellow in colour, and borne in masses. These are followed by attractive, small, orange **fruits** shaped like small apricots which split open when ripe to reveal deep red, sticky **seeds.** A tree laden with these colourful fruits is a lovely sight during autumn and winter.

This tree is easily cultivated, particularly in light soils, and tolerates much wetter conditions than it usually encounters in its natural environment. It is particularly ornamental as a weeping specimen tree, and should receive more favourable consideration than it does, as a garden subject. It is slow growing, but permanent.

"Native Apricot" is protected by law in South Australia.

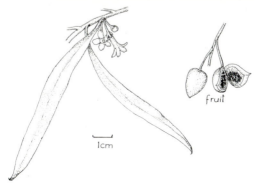
fruit

SWEET PITTOSPORUM, MOCK ORANGE

Pittosporum undulatum Vent.　　　　　　　PITTOSPORACEAE

A commonly cultivated tree, "Sweet Pittosporum" is an inhabitant of the sub-tropical to temperate forests of the east coast extending south from Brisbane to north-east Victoria. Except for *P. phylliraeoides* (see p. 202) all species of the genus in Australia are found in the high rainfall sub-tropical to tropical areas, usually growing dense and bushy, under 14 m in height.

"Sweet Pittosporum" is a dense, bushy crowned tree up to **10 m high,** often with foliage to near ground level and grey **bark** rather like coarse sandpaper. The laurel-like **leaves** are dark glossy green, paler underneath, with wavy margins, and occur in whorls at the end of the twigs. The tree flowers in September when the terminal bunches of pale-cream, bell-shaped **flowers** spread their strong fragrance into the surrounding areas. The 12 mm diameter **fruits** (or berries) which follow are in handsome clusters, a bright orange in colour, and open to reveal sticky, red insides and black **seeds.**

This tree is easily grown where rainfall is moderate, and has been extensively cultivated in such places as Adelaide where it has regenerated naturally in certain Hills districts. It can be grown under large established trees, and is useful for this reason as well as being a good ornamental evergreen shade or specimen tree. If properly planted it can also make a useful clipped hedge. Two other east coast pittosporums have occasionally been cultivated. *P. revolutum* Ait. is a dense and compact, attractive, small tree found from Gippsland in Victoria to southern Queensland. **Leaves** are light green, lance-shaped, and covered with rust-coloured hairs on the undersurface. The small, attractive, yellow **flowers** are followed by egg-shaped **fruits** up to 2·5 cm long containing red, sticky **seeds.** *P. rhombifolium* A. Cunn. is another attractive, but rarely grown tree of up to **14 m in height,** found from northern New South Wales to Proserpine in Queensland. The **leaves** are broad (rhomboid), glossy, and toothed. The numerous terminal clusters of small, pear-shaped, bright orange **fruits** which are very ornamental during autumn and early winter are a feature of the tree. Both species prefer non-limy, moist soils, and some protection.

P. undulatum   1cm   fruit

BROWN PINE, SHE PINE, ILLAWARRA PLUM
Podocarpus elatus R.Br. PODOCARPACEAE

"Brown Pine" is a fairly large conifer of the coastal scrub forests which extend from the Illawarra district of New South Wales northwards to Cairns in Queensland. Mature trees reach **45 m** or more under these conditions, and are a conspicuous feature of the predominantly dark green jungle with their very pale green, soft new foliage.

A genus which is widespread throughout the Southern Hemisphere (there are six Australian species), the *Podocarpus* differs from other conifers by its absence of woody, seed-bearing cones. These are borne on fleshy scales.

The younger trees of "Brown Pine" often form a broadly conical-shaped and compact evergreen with shiny green foliage to the ground. The **trunk** is seldom buttressed but often irregularly indented or fluted. Dark brown **bark** is thin and finely fissured. The sharply pointed **leaves** are narrow and long, alternate, and on very short stalks with a glossy upper surface. Male and female **flower spikes** are small, and on separate trees.

The female trees produce **fruits** consisting of a fleshy plum-shaped receptacle of a purplish colour, and about 2·5 cm in diameter. These are edible and can be made into a tasty jelly. They bear a **seed** at their apex similar to that of the "Native Cherry" (*Exocarpos*).

The tough, durable **timber** is golden-brown, silky textured, and particularly attractive for featured woodwork.

This is a fine, ornamental tree, best suited to rich, moist, non-alkaline soils. It requires some protection.

BLACK PINE *P. amarus* Blume is a similar tree with dark **bark,** native to the Atherton Tableland district of northern Queensland, and extending to New Guinea and nearby islands. The receptacles on the **fruits** are not as developed as those of "Brown Pine," but the **seeds** are red and twice the size.

MOUNTAIN BROWN PINE *P. lawrencei* Hook. f. (*P. alpina* R. Br.) is a small, gnarled, broad-leaved conifer from alpine (altitudes exceeding 1000 m) regions of Victoria, New South Wales, and Tasmania. It bears red, succulent **fruits.**

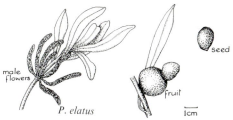

P. elatus

DEEP YELLOW-WOOD, TULIP SATINWOOD

Rhodosphaera rhodanthema Engl.　　　ANACARDIACEAE

"Deep Yellow-wood" is a tropical rain forest tree of the coastal areas of New South Wales, north of the Clarence River, and Queensland, where it extends some 160 km inland.

Compared with many of the trees found in these luxuriant forests, this is only a small tree usually under **16 m in height,** although it sometimes grows taller. In cultivation it is a shapely, rather widespreading tree up to **10 m high** with handsome pinnate foliage; it makes an ideal garden shade and specimen tree for a well-watered lawn.

The **bark** of the tree is rough, grey or brown in colour, and very scaly. When cut it is a bright red or pink and exudes a sticky white gum.

The **leaves** are alternate, and pinnate, and are made up of 4–13 leaflets arranged in opposite pairs, each leaflet 5–7 cm long. The young shoots are very downy, being covered with rust-coloured hairs, which sometimes persist to the underside of the mature leaves and give the foliage a brownish tinge. The **branches** are spotted with small raised dots (lenticels).

The small **flowers** which are bright red with yellow anthers are borne in large terminal panicles in spring, when they make a showy display. These are followed by masses of attractive, grape-like bunches of berries or **fruits** which ripen to a shining, reddish-brown colour. Each fruit is about 12 mm in diameter. When dried they are excellent subjects for floral art arrangement.

When first cut, the heartwood is a bright yellow. This gives the tree its common name. The **timber** is sometimes used for fancy woodwork and polishes to an attractive pale yellow colour.

"Deep Yellow-wood" is an ornamental tree which grows to a good shape and size for average suburban gardens. Unfortunately it is not well known and has not received much attention as a cultivated tree. It requires plenty of water and prefers rich soils, but is adaptable, and grows well as far south as Adelaide.

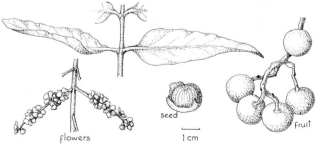

flowers   seed   1 cm   fruit

QUANDONG, NATIVE PEACH

Santalum acuminatum DC.   SANTALACEAE
(syn. *Eucarya acuminata* Spr. et Summerh.).

Although well known by name, "Quandong" has become quite rare in many places where it once grew freely. In South Australia, in particular, both the "Quandong" and "Bitter Quandong" are protected plants, although it is doubtful if this law is respected by many citizens. It is an inhabitant of low to moderate rainfall and light soil areas of temperate Australia, and is still commonly encountered in Western Australia. "Quandong" belongs to the "Sandalwood" family, all of which are root parasites being nourished by sucker-like attachments which feed on the roots of host plants. They are related to the "Mistletoes" which are also parasites (see *Nuytsia*, p. 198).

It is only a **small compact tree,** often a shrub, with long, lanceolate rather fleshy, pale grey-green **leaves** on slender **branchlets.** The small white **flowers** in terminal panicles are insignificant, but are followed by attractive succulent, rounded red **fruits** on long pendulous stalks usually in summer. These fruits are edible, and although rather sour when eaten fresh, can be made into excellent jam and preserves. They contain a round, light brown, roughly pitted stone (endocarp), often used for children's playthings. The **kernel** is edible and very oily with a burning taste; emus love it, and play an important part in spreading the seed. The **timber** is also oily and was used by the Aborigines for creating fire by friction.

BITTER QUANDONG *S. murrayanum* C. A. Gardn. is a very similar tree with drooping foliage from the same habitat, but distinguished by its smaller **flowers** which appear in axillary panicles, the brownish, bitter **fruits,** and the stone which in this case is only slightly pitted. **FRAGRANT SANDALWOOD** *S. spicatum* (R. Br.) A. DC. is a crooked, **rough-barked** tree growing **to 8 m** found in the Flinders Ranges and northern South Australia, and commonly in southern Western Australia. The tiny **flowers** in axillary panicles are fragrant, as is the wood, which has been exported for use as incense in Chinese temples. It is an excellent fuel and is used for firing brick kilns. **PLUM BUSH** *S. lanceolatum* R. Br. from inland Australia sometimes reaches tree proportions. It has glaucous **leaves,** small purple **fruits,** and aromatic wood.

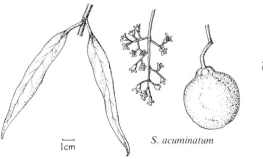

S. acuminatum

UMBRELLA TREE

Schefflera actinophylla Harms. ARALIACEAE
(syn. *Brassaia actinophylla* Endl.).

"Umbrella Tree" comes from the rain forests of northern New South Wales and Queensland where it grows **14–16 m** tall, sometimes beginning its life as an epiphyte in the branches of a host tree.

The tree is very adaptable, and is extensively cultivated, seldom growing much larger than **about 8 m high,** particularly in the cooler more temperate areas where it can be grown easily.

In cultivation it usually forms several slender main stems arising from the root stock. The large palmate **leaves** are attached by very long stalks (40–70 cm long) which are arranged alternately around these main stems. Each leaf comprises (usually 12–15) large leathery leaflets of a deep lustrous green on individual stalks several centimetres long. These are attached to the end of the main stalk in a circular, umbrella-like formation. The younger leaves appearing at the tops of each stem are a much paler, shining green.

The bright red attractive **flowers** occur on long upright spikes. Their arrangement resembles the tentacles of an octopus, and in Hawaii the tree is known as "Octopus Tree." The flowers change to black as the **seed pods** develop. Away from its native warm climate "Umbrella Tree" does not flower regularly, although in some years it is quite free flowering, dependent on seasonal conditions.

Not fussy as regards soils, "Umbrella Tree" is easily grown if given plenty of water and a sunny position. Areas where frosts are severe should be avoided. It is a tree requiring very little attention, seldom producing any vigorous unwanted branches requiring pruning, and causing no problem with leaf drop.

This tree has many uses and is a fine "structural" plant for producing a tropical effect in the garden. In the more tropical parts of Queensland and New South Wales it is successfully grown as a street tree.

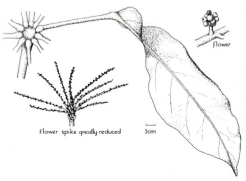

Flower spike greatly reduced   1cm   flower

WHEEL OF FIRE, FIRE-WHEEL TREE

Stenocarpus sinuatus Endl. PROTEACEAE

"Wheel of Fire Tree" is an upright, non-spreading tree, well known in cultivation, where it grows quite successfully in much cooler climates than its native habitat. It is a tropical rain forest species of the east coast, extending from northern New South Wales to the Atherton Tableland in Queensland; it often grows in dense jungle where it reaches **14–35 m in height.**

The tree has a slender grey or dark brown **trunk** with wrinkled **bark.** It is densely clothed with rich green, glossy foliage and soft, downy, bronze-coloured new growth. The large **leaves** are extremely variable, and of firm texture. Some are entire usually with wavy margins, others slightly divided, or deeply lobed.

It is the curiously shaped **flowers** that are the conspicuous feature of this tree. They are borne in large, prominent clusters during autumn and early winter when they make a spectacular display. The flower is 4–7 cm long and arranged in a circular fashion like the spokes of a wheel. Each flower (or spoke) is a bright scarlet with an enlarged, globular apex, coloured yellow.

The **fruits** (follicles) are dry, boat-shaped capsules containing winged **seeds** from which the tree is easily propagated.

"Wheel of Fire Tree" is a fine, ornamental flowering tree **seldom exceeding 14 m when cultivated.** In its juvenile stage it can also be used as a tub house plant. The tree requires good soils in a climate with warm to hot summers, and plenty of moisture for best results. In southern Australia it is slow growing, but permanent, and is a most distinctive addition to any garden.

SCRUB BEEFWOOD *S. salignus* R. Br. is a common rain forest tree of mainly New South Wales, where it reaches **nearly 33 m.** In cultivation it is only a small, densely branched tree, requiring similar conditions to the "Wheel of Fire Tree." The **leaves** are narrowly elliptical with 3 prominent longitudinal (or striate) nerves. **Flowers** are white in attractive small rosettes, and **fruits,** long bean-like follicles. The **timber** is considered very ornamental.

S. sinuatus

S. salignus

TURPENTINE TREE

Syncarpia procera Domin. MYRTACEAE
(syn. *S. laurifolia* Ten. syn. *S. glomulifera* Nied.).

There are four Australian species of the genus *Syncarpia*, and they are known as "Turpentines." The name is derived from the orange-red resin which resembles turpentine, and protects the timber from termites and borers.

S. procera is a towering shaft-like timber tree, usually **30–70 m high.** A species abundant in the eastern coastal scrub forests of Queensland and New South Wales, it prefers deep fertile soils in valleys and depressions, although it is found in many other soils and situations in these areas.

It is a handsome, upright, somewhat conical tree, particularly when young, with a brown, persistent, thick and fibrous, stringy **bark. Leaves** are oval-oblong, 5–9 cm long, opposite, and dark green with dense woolly whitish hairs on the underside. The creamy **flowers** which appear in spring, are in dense, globular heads on stout stalks and are much loved by bees. **Fruits** consist of 3-celled capsules united into a small head and containing numerous tiny **seeds.**

Timber of the "Turpentines" is particularly valuable for its durability both in exposed situations and in sea water construction, as it is resistant to marine borers. It is a dark pinkish-brown in colour, hard, tough, and heavy, with many uses besides those mentioned.

S. hillii Bail. which is also known as "Peebeen" is native to Fraser Island off the Queensland coast. It has longer **leaves** than the preceding species, up to 12 cm long, but is very similar in general appearance.

S. leptopetala F. Muell. is a much smaller tree of the eastern scrub forests, **seldom exceeding about 16 m in height.** The wavy **leaves** are yellowish-green in colour giving the tree an attractive overall effect. Flowering when very young it forms a useful street tree for sub-tropical regions.

The fourth species, *S. subargentea* C. T. White, is a tall, shaft-like forest tree from Queensland only, with a thin, smooth **bark.**

These latter two species are also referred to as *Choricarpia*.

All the "Turpentines" form ornamental trees which are sometimes cultivated in sub-tropical areas.

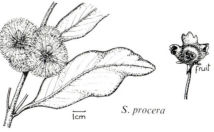

S. procera
1cm
fruit

BRUSH CHERRY

Syzygium paniculatum Gaertn. MYRTACEAE

Often called a "Lilly Pilly," the syzygiums and the closely related eugenias are, as a group, perhaps the most frequently cultivated of all Australia's rain forest trees. Although of varying habit, they are all shapely, dense, evergreen trees with glossy leaves, and usually colourful, attractive fruits.

"Brush Cherry" is probably the hardiest species of the genus, and is often seen in gardens. It is found naturally in the brush forests from Illawarra to Atherton, often hanging over streams, and has been called "Creek Lilly Pilly." Under these conditions the tree is often irregular in growth, but in cultivation it is an upright, symmetrical tree, **10–16 m high,** with a dark, scaly **bark,** and very handsome appearance. **Leaves** in opposite pairs, are glossy, lance-shaped, 5–8 cm long. New shoots are reddish and shiny, and add to the tree's attraction. The fluffy, cream-coloured **flowers** are in abundant and attractive panicles in November–December but the **fruits** which appear in late summer and autumn provide the main display. These are bright purplish-red, oval, and variable in size, occurring in dense, cherry-like bunches. Each fruit contains a solitary **seed** surrounded by fleshy pulp which is succulent and edible, but not particularly tasty, being rather acid in flavour. A well-formed tree loaded down by these coloured fruits, is a very handsome sight. **LILLY PILLY** *Eugenia smithii* Poir. is a very similar tree found in rain forests from Victoria to Cape York Peninsula, and in the Northern Territory. The **flowers** are less conspicuous, and **fruits** are smaller and egg-shaped to elliptic, usually a purplish colour. This species is also extensively cultivated. Several other cultivated species, all native to the east coast, are: **RED APPLE** *Eugenia brachyandra* Maid. & Betch. A tall, handsome tree with showy masses of light red **fruits. SMALL-LEAVED WATER GUM** *S. leuhmannii* Johnson. A large densely foliaged tree with reddish, pear-shaped **fruits. WEEPING MYRTLE** *Syzygium floribundum* F. Muell. A large, **thick trunked** tree with rough fissured **bark** and somewhat drooping foliage. **BLUE-FRUITED LILLY PILLY** *S. coolminianum* Johnson. Only a small tree with numerous, bluish, urn-shaped **fruits** which make a fine display. Syzygiums are usually quick growing, and require non-limy, moist soils for best results.

Syzygium paniculatum · fruit · *Eugenia smithii*

TREE WARATAH, GIPPSLAND WARATAH
Telopea oreades F. Muell. PROTEACEAE

The "Waratahs" are one of Australia's most famous wildflowers. The name is derived from "telopas," meaning distance, referring to the great distance from which the flowers are visible. "Tree Waratah" is native to east Gippsland in Victoria and to the south-east coast of New South Wales where it grows to a small, shapely tree **10–14 m high** at its best. It favours well-drained soils in sheltered places with an annual rainfall exceeding 750 mm.

It has a thin, smooth, dark brown **bark** on a **trunk** never more than 50 cm in diameter. The smooth, dark green, lanceolate **leaves,** 10–20 cm long, are rather thick, narrowed at the base, and often with recurved margins. Although not as large as the famous "New South Wales Waratah," the unusual dark red **flowers** are showy, appearing in terminal clusters which collectively look like a large rounded flower about 10 cm in diameter. It blooms in summer.

Often found lining the banks of streams, the tree can be viewed from nearby hillsides. Their masses of red flowers are a delight in springtime.

Fruits are curved, leathery follicles, and the **timber** is light brown with an attractive grain.

The genus consists of three Australian species.

TASMANIAN WARATAH *T. truncata* R. Br. is a small, erect, or spreading tree or shrub, up to **8 m high,** but usually less, common in the mountain ranges of Tasmania. The **leaves** which are 5–12 cm long are smaller than those of "Tree Waratah" but otherwise it is similar to that species. It flowers in December, and has a yellow flowering form as well as the usual red.

NEW SOUTH WALES WARATAH *T. speciosissima* R. Br. is the best known species, being extensively cultivated for cut flowers where conditions are suitable. It is usually a tall, slender, rather stiff shrub with handsome leathery, lobed **leaves,** and magnificent heads of large, crimson **flowers** which last for weeks when cut. It is a common plant in the Blue Mountains near Sydney and is the floral emblem of New South Wales. The shrub flowers in late spring to summer.

All the "Waratahs" dislike lime or alkaline soils, and seem to grow best in rather poor, stony, well-drained soils.

Photograph by courtesy of R. N. Auchterlonie

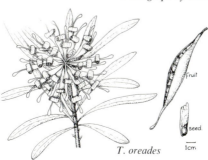

T. oreades

RED CEDAR

Toona australis Harms. MELIACEAE
(syn. *Cedrela toona* var. *australis* C.DC.).

"Red Cedar" is a giant, handsome, deciduous tree, native to the rain forests of the east coast, from south of Sydney to Cape York Peninsula in northern Queensland. Once the pride of the Queensland rain forests and much sought after for its fragrant, soft, highly-figured timber, the tree has now become rare, and is seldom seen growing naturally, except perhaps in inaccessible country. The early colonists opened up many new areas in search of this tree, and unfortunately have almost eliminated one of these forests' finest assets.

"Red Cedar" is closely related to the Indian "Toona Tree." It is known to reach **heights of 70 m** with a **trunk** 3 m in diameter, well buttressed at the base. **Bark** is brown or grey, scaly, and is shed in fibrous flakes leaving a smooth, reddish **trunk** beneath. Although tall and upright, the tree is well branched with a shapely, medium-sized crown. The handsome, pinnate **leaves** are alternate, and consist of 3–8 pairs of leaflets, each leaflet 4–10 cm in length, and converging to a long point at the apex. **Flowers** are small and sweetly perfumed, blooming in spring in large panicles at the ends of the branchlets, and are white or pale pink in colour. The **fruit** is a dry, oval capsule, about 2·5 cm long, 5-valved, and containing long winged **seeds.**

The **timber** of the "Red Cedar" is soft, light, and durable, beautifully figured, and much valued for ornamental woodwork, furniture, and other uses. It polishes to a rich red colour which is enhanced as it ages.

This tree is occasionally cultivated in parks and large gardens where it forms a large, shapely tree exceeding 33 m in height. It grows rapidly when planted in the tropics, but is often retarded by attacks from the Red Cedar Tip Moth. The tree is quite successful as far south as Adelaide, but requires deep, rich soils and abundant water.

Siehe GEO, Nr. 16/4/1994

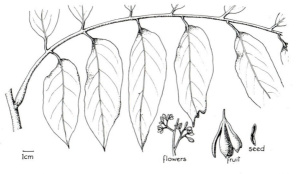
flowers   fruit   seed
1cm

BRUSH BOX
Tristania conferta R.Br.
MYRTACEAE

Well known in cultivation and a useful timber tree, "Brush Box" naturally occurs in the sub-tropical forests of New South Wales north of Newcastle, and southern Queensland, with some isolated occurrences as far north as the Atherton Tableland. It is usually an intermediate species bordering true rain forests, where it prefers protected valleys and river flats with rich alluvial soils, although it is sometimes found at elevations to 1000 m. Rainfall is 750–1500 mm.

The tree is naturally tall, **40–50 m,** with a straight, well-formed, shaft-like **trunk,** 1–2 m in diameter. Under colder more temperate conditions, where it is frequently grown, particularly as a street tree, "Brush Box" is a much smaller tree, **10–15 m in height,** with a symmetrical and dense conical crown; sometimes sadly abused when the tree is trained to grow beneath overhead service wires.

The **bark** is rough and scaly at the base but smooth on the upper **trunk** and **branches,** where the orange or dark brown colour contrasts well with the dark green shiny foliage. Juvenile **leaves** are soft and hairy, but mature to a glossy green with dull undersurface. These are alternate, rather large and elliptical, with a prominent midrib. **Flowers** are white and up to 4 cm across, appearing in axillary cymes with 5 stamens united into feathery bundles. They appear in spring. The bell-shaped **fruits** are 3-celled and reminiscent of those of the eucalypt. The ornamental **timber** is prized for hardwood floors and other uses.

"Brush Box" is a dense, ornamental evergreen which grows well in Perth and Adelaide, as well as in the eastern States. It is best suited to better class, moist soils, and resents limestone.

Two other Australian species sometimes cultivated are **WATER GUM** *T. neriifolia* R. Br., a small tree distinguished by its opposite **leaves** and more or less localized habitat from Cooma to the Blue Mountains and Port Jackson districts, and **KANUKA** or **WATER GUM** *T. laurina* R. Br., a tree growing **to 20 m.** They are both **rough-barked,** ornamental trees with masses of dainty yellow **flowers** in summer, and usually favour watercourses or damp situations. "Kanuka" extends from Queensland to Gippsland in Victoria and is also native to New Zealand.

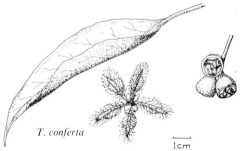

T. conferta

1cm

GLOSSARY OF TERMS USED

adpressed or appressed: Pressed close to, or lying flat against something. Referring to the leaves on the stems.
alternate: Placed at different levels—referring to the position of each leaf on the branchlets.
anther: The pollen bearing part of a stamen.
axil: The angle between a part and its parent body—e.g. a leaf and the main stem of a plant.
bipinnate: Pinnate leaves in which the leaflets are again divided into secondary leaflets—e.g. the leaves of many species of Acacia.
calcareous: Referring to a soil of limestone origin.
calyx: Primary sterile appendage of a receptacle consisting of two or more united carpels.
capsule: A dry fruit formed from a multi-carpelled ovary.
carpel: The female part of a flower which bears the ovules—one or more carpels comprise the ovary.
catkin: A spike formed from a pendulous rachis (primary axis) bearing unisexual flowers.
cladode: A leaf-like stem functioning as a true leaf.
corymb: An inflorescence with flowers approximately at one level due to varying pedicel lengths. The lowermost or outside flowers which open first have longer pedicels than the upper ones.
cotyledon: Primary leaf developed in a seed; seed leaf.
cyme: A broad, rather flat-topped inflorescence with the first formed flower in the centre opening first. Subsequent flowers are produced by growth from a lateral bud.
deciduous: Shedding of leaves or bark at the end of the growing season.
decorticate: To shed bark.
decussate: Arranged in opposite pairs, each pair at right angles to its following pair—referring to the leaf arrangement on a stem.
disc: A small development of the receptacle around the ovary.
drupe: A succulent fruit with a hard stone enclosing a single seed.
elliptical: (Shape of leaf.) Oval, tapered to rounded ends.

endemic: Native to a particular country or region.

endocarp: The stone surrounding a kernel or seed; the inner wall of a pericarp or drupe—the pericarp being the fleshy fruit or wall surrounding the endocarp.

entire: Without toothing or divisions—referring to the leaves.

epiphyte: A plant growing on a host plant with no connection to the soil, and depending on decayed matter from the host for its nutrients.

falcate: Sickle-shaped; flat, curving, and tapering to a point.

fastigiate: Conical, or pyramid shaped—as many pines or conifers.

filament: The stalk of an anther.

fissured: Narrow cleft or opening (in the bark of a tree).

follicle: A dry fruit containing more than one seed and which splits open along a lateral line on one side only—e.g. the fruit of Grevillea.

funicle: The basal stalk of an ovule or seed.

glabrous: Without hairs, smooth.

glaucous: Covered with a whitish or bluish bloom or powder, often giving an ashy or blue-green effect.

hoary: Covered with short, dense, whitish or pale grey hairs.

hypanthium: A floral cup or tube.

imbricate: Overlapping.

inflorescence: The flower bearing system.

lanceolate: Lance-shaped, widest below the middle and tapered to an acute apex, the length at least three times the width.

lateritic: Referring to a laterite or ironstone soil.

leaflet: The ultimate segment of a compound leaf.

lenticel: The space or pore in the outer tissue of most plants.

linear: (Shape of leaf.) Long and narrow with more or less parallel sides

lobe: The rounded segment of a structure—e.g. some leaves are divided into several lobes.

midrib: The main central vein of a leaf.

mucro: A sharp terminal point.

nerve: Refer vein.

node: The region of the stem from which the leaf or root system arises.

obovate: Reserved ovate; egg shaped with narrow end attached to stalk.

operculum: A cap or lid (covering the flowers of Eucalyptus).

opposite: Arranged in line but on opposite sides of a node—referring to the leaf arrangement on a branchlet.

ovary: Part of the flower which contains the ovules.

ovate: Egg-shaped; broadest below the mid-line with a rounded apex.

ovule: The site of egg-cell or seed formation in a plant. The young seed in the ovary prior to fertilisation.

palmate: Arranged in a fan-shaped formation.

panicle: A branched cluster of flowers with pedicels or stalks.

pedicel: The stalk of an individual flower.

peduncle: The stalk of a cluster of flowers, or of an individual flower if this is the only member of the inflorescence.

pedunculate: Having a peduncle; being attached by a peduncle.
petiole: The stalk of a leaf.
phyllode: A flattened leaf stalk or petiole which functions as a leaf.
pinnae: Divisions or leaflets of a pinnate leaf.
pinnate: With leaflets arranged on both sides of a central stalk (rachis) in feather-like fashion.
pollard: To cut off or prune the whole crown of a tree.
pubescent: Covered with short, soft hairs or down.
pungent: Terminating in a stiff, sharp point.
pyramidal: Pyramid or cone-shaped.
raceme: A simple inflorescence with a central axis producing stalked flowers along its length.
rachis: The primary axis of an inflorescence, or a compound leaf.
receptacle: Tip of a floral stem bearing floral units which form the flower.
recurved: Bent backwards.
reflexed: Bent or turned sharply backwards.
rhomboid or rhombic: Rhomboid-shaped, resembling an equilateral parallelogram with acute angles.
scabrous: Rough to touch.
sclerophyll: A closed plant community dominated by evergreen sclerophyllous trees (trees with hard textured leaves such as Eucalyptus).
serrated: With saw-toothed edges or margins.
sessile: Without a stalk.
stamen: Part of a male flower consisting of a filament (stalk) and a pollen bearing anther.
stigma: The part of a carpel which receives the pollen.
stipule: The lateral part of a leaf borne near or at the base of the leaf.
striate: Fine longitudinal lines, such as the vein structure of some leaves.
style: The sterile part of a carpel connecting a stigma to its ovary.
terete: Needle-like; shaped like a narrow tapered shaft.
terminal: At the tip or end.
testa: Seed coat.
tomentum: A mat or covering of dense, woolly hairs.
trifoliate: Describing a compound leaf which bears three leaflets.
umbel: An arrangement of pedicellate flowers arising from a common point of the floral axis or peduncle.
umbrageous: Umbrella-like.
unisexual: Of one sex — e.g. a flower where only one sex is present.
valve: The segment of a fruit which naturally splits open at maturity, and usually containing seeds.
vein: Strand of conducting tissue in the structure of a leaf.
venation: The method of vein arrangement.
viable: Capable of development — referring to the germination of seeds.
whorl: Arranged in radial fashion around an axis — e.g. a radial group of leaves or flowers at a node.

REFERENCE BOOKS

AUSTRALIAN PLANTS—*Journal of Society for Growing Australian Plants*
AUSTRALIAN PLANTS FOR THE GARDEN—*Thistle Y. Harris*
AUSTRALIAN RAIN FOREST TREES—*W. D. Francis*
FLORA OF SOUTH AUSTRALIA—*J. M. Black*
FOREST FLORA OF NEW SOUTH WALES—*J. H. Maiden*
FOREST TREES OF AUSTRALIA—*Forest & Timber Bureau of Australia*
GROWING AUSTRALIAN PLANTS—*Noel Lothian and Ivan Holliday*
HANDBOOK OF FOREST TREES FOR VICTORIAN FORESTERS—*A. J. Ewart*
HONEY FLORA OF SOUTH EAST QUEENSLAND—*S. T. Blake and C. Roff*
KEY TO THE EUCALYPTS—*W. F. Blakely*
NATIVE TREES OF AUSTRALIA—*J. W. Audas*
THE PRACTICAL HOME GARDENER—*T. R. N. Lothian*
TREES OF AUSTRALIA—*H. Oakman*
TREES OF NEW SOUTH WALES—*R. H. Anderson*
TREES OF WESTERN AUSTRALIA—*C. A. Gardner—Publication by W.A. Department of Agriculture*
TREE PLANTING GUIDE FOR RURAL SOUTH AUSTRALIA—*C. D. Boomsma—Publication by S.A. Woods & Forests Department*
VICTORIAN HONEY FLORA—*Victorian Department of Agriculture*